Best Wishes

[signature]

Feb. 2022

CONVERSATIONS WITH MY FATHER

Forty years on, a daughter responds

by Moneeza Hashmi

928.954 Hashmi, Moneeza
Conversations With My Father / Moneeza Hashmi. - Lahore: Sang-e-Meel Publications, 2022.
160pp.
1. Memoirs - Biography - Literature
I. Title.

2022
Published by
Afzaal Ahmad
Sang-e-Meel Publications
Lahore.

ISBN-10: 969-35-3406-9

ISBN-13: 978-969-35-3406-1

Sang-e-Meel Publications
25 - Lower Mall, Lahore 54000, Pakistan.
+92 42 37220100 - +92 42 37228143
www.sangemeel.com - email: smp@sangemeel.com

آنے والے دنوں کے
سفیروں کے نام

DEDICATED TO MY GRANDSONS

Hamzah Ali Hashmi
Mahir Ali Hashmi
Ahmer Aftab Hashmi

Photo credits to **Athar Shahzad** and **Bhatti studio**

Table of Content

ایک لحاظ سے میں ان خطوط کو روحانی کہتی ہوں، کیونکہ ان میں کوئی ترسیل کا ذریعہ نہیں، کوئی نامہ بر نہیں اور کوئی پتہ بھی نہیں (جنت کا کوئی پتہ ہوتا بھی نہیں ہے)۔مگر یہ یقین اپنی جگہ مکمل ہے کہ جسے لکھے گئے ہیں اُسے ملیں گے ضرور۔۔۔

تمھاری تحریر میں تم نے ایک ہلکا سا غم بھی چھپا رکھا ہے۔اور وہ غم ہے اپنے شاندار باپ کے ساتھ وقت نہ گزارنے کا۔۔۔ان سے زیادہ باتیں نہ کرنے کا۔۔۔اور جب تم اپنے بچوں کو ان کے بچوں سے باتیں کرتے دیکھتی ہو تب تمھیں اپنی محرومی کا احساس ہوتا ہے۔لیکن تم خود ہی اپنی اداسی کو ان لمحوں سے دور کر دیتی ہو جو اُن کے قُرب میں تمھیں میسر آئے۔۔۔تم فوراً اُس چائینیز ہوٹل میں چلی جاتی ہو۔تم اپنے پسندیدہ کھانے کھاتی ہو۔۔۔اور وہ تم کو بس دیکھتے رہتے ہیں۔۔۔تمہارا سری نگر جانے والا خط۔۔۔اس مکان کو دیکھنے کی تمنّا جہاں تم پیدا ہوئی تھیں۔تمہاری مستعدی اور جستجو کی تصویر دکھاتا ہے، پھر شہر شہر گھومنے کی تفصیلات، اپنی نوکری کے نشیب و فراز، بس یوں لگتا ہے تم سُنا رہی ہو اور فیض صاحب سُن رہے ہیں۔اور تم اپنی زندگی کو اُن کی آنکھوں سے دیکھ رہی ہو۔۔۔

میزو مجھے پورا یقین ہے کہ تمھارے خط فیض صاحب تک ضرور پہنچ گئے ہوں گے۔اور اُن کے چہرے پر مسکراہٹ بھی آتی ہوگی۔۔۔اور پھر اُنہوں نے اپنے مخصوص انداز سے کہا ہوگا۔۔۔

'ہمارے جانے کے بعد ہماری میزو واقعی بڑی ہوگئی ہے۔اب تو اسے سوئچ off کرنا اور on کرنا بھی آگیا ہے۔' پھر اُنہوں نے سگریٹ بجھا دیا ہوگا۔معلوم نہیں جنت میں سگریٹ کی اجازت ہے کہ نہیں۔۔۔اور اگر نہیں ہے تو ہوسکتا ہے انھیں اسپیشل پرمیشن مل گئی ہو۔

تم کو بہت بہت دعائیں اور پیار

خیر طلب

زہرا آپا

پیش لفظ

میزو

بہت پیار اور دعائیں

یہ تمہاری محبت ہے کہ تم نے اپنی کتاب پر مجھ سے لکھنے کو کہا۔ یہ کتاب چونکہ خطوط سے مرتب کی گئی ہے اس لئے میں نے سوچا تم کو خط ہی لکھ دوں۔ ویسے بھی مجھے مقدمہ یا دیباچہ لکھنا تو آتا نہیں۔۔۔

جیسا کہ ہم سب جانتے ہیں، خطوط ہمارے ادب کی بہت دلفریب صنفِ سُخن ہے۔

دو آدمیوں کے درمیان ان کے تعلقات کو بے کم و کاست واضح کرتی ہے، بہ ظاہر لکھنے والا کوئی ایک ہوتا ہے۔۔۔

ہم ابھی تک **'صلیبیں مرے دریچے میں'** کے نشہ سے باہر نہیں نکلے تھے، کہ ایلس کے خطوط سامنے آگئے۔۔۔ سچے اور سادہ۔۔۔ اور اب تمہارے خطوط۔۔۔ اِس کتاب کی انفرادیت یہ ہے کہ یہ خطوط اُس ہستی کو لکھے جا رہے ہیں، جو اَب اِس دنیا میں نہیں۔ مگر اِس ہستی کے لئے 'نہیں' کا لفظ درست نہیں۔ کیونکہ وہ تو ہے۔ اگر ہم سب کے لئے ہے تو تمہارے لئے تو یقیناً ہے۔

فیض صاحب نے جو کچھ تمہارے اور تمہارے بچوں کے لئے لکھا، اِن میں فیض صاحب کی کم آمیزی نمایاں ہے جو ان کی گفتگو میں بھی تھی۔ مگر محبت اور خیال کی خوشبو سے مہکے یہ خط دل موہ لیتے ہیں۔

تمہارے خط انگریزی میں ہیں، اور فیض صاحب کے اردو میں۔۔۔ یہ امتزاج بھی اس کتاب کی صفات میں شامل ہے۔ تمہارے خطوط میں طرزِ تحریر اور الفاظ کا چناؤ تمہاری شخصیت کے آئینہ دار ہیں۔۔۔ جس زبان میں سوچو اسی میں لکھنا چاہیئے۔۔۔ (ویسے بھی تمہاری مادری زبان تو انگریزی ہے)۔ تمہارے لکھے خطوط میں صرف اطلاعات نہیں ہیں، واقعات، خوشیاں، غم سب ہی کچھ تو ہے۔ اگر میں خطوط کے بارے میں لکھنا شروع کروں تو پھر پوری ایک کتاب بن جائے گی۔۔۔ اِس لئے اشارتاً صرف چند خطوط کی بات کروں گی۔

Foreward

Mizu

Love and prayers for you.

It has to be your love and affection that you ask me to write a piece for your book. Since this is a collection of letters, I thought I might as well write one too. More so because I do not know how to write a foreword or preface…Besides we all know that letter writing is one of the most beautiful traditions of our literary tradition. It is such an amazingly accurate exposition of the relationship between two people, though the writer is but one person on his own.

We had still not got over the charisma of "Saleebayn Meray Dareechoon Main" that Alys' letters came up …heartfelt and unaffected. And now your letters. The significance of this book is that these are letters addressed to a person who is no longer in this world. But wait, for how can we use the past tense, the phrase 'not in this world' for him because he simply 'is'. And if for all of us he 'is', then for you, his daughter, even today he is more 'is'.

Faiz Saheb's signature precision of expression, something that also marked his conversations, shows through in what he has written for you and for your children. Yet these letters seep into the heart for the affection and fragrance they exude. You write in English and Faiz Saheb writes in Urdu…a fusion that enriches the allure of this book. The language and style of your letters images your personality …of course one must write in the language one thinks in…(as it is, your mother tongue is English). They contain not only everyday news but the tiny joys and blues et al. If I start writing about all the letters this will turn into an entire book. So I shall talk about a
select few.

At one level I consider these letters almost spiritual because they carry no timeline, no inkling about the carrier and no address (paradise too is without an address) and yet they come with the conviction that they will reach the person to whom they are being written to.
You have camouflaged a gentle sorrow too in your writing…the lament of not having spent time with your great father. The regret of not having had lengthier conversations with him; a regret enhanced when you see your own children talking to their children. But the very second instant you fight free of this regret when you recount the precious time spent in his company. You walk into that Chinese restaurant, you order your favourite dishes….and he simple watches over you. That letter in which you mention visiting Srinagar, your desire to visit the house you were born in…all show strength of purpose and searchings. Then your travel experiences around the world's many cities, the highs and lows of your career, every word is a syllable directly spoken and directly heard…you are looking at your life through his eyes.

Mizu I am confident your letters must have reached Faiz Saheb and his face would have been lit up in a smile…and then in his own special style he would have said, 'My Mizu has really grown up in my absence. Sure she has learnt how to swap the on and off of light switches.' Then he would have rubbed off his cigarette. I wonder if one can smoke in Paradise? If not then he just might have been granted that permission.

Lots of love and prayers for you

Your's affectionately
Zehra Apa

The Beginning

So what took me so long to get this book started?

So what took me so long to get this book started?

A good question!
Firstly, I am still struggling with myself, having lived in the "semi" limelight for most of my life. Partly as the daughter of a great poet; partly as the sister of a great painter; partly on management posts of the only TV public broadcaster in Pakistan; partly as the only woman to head the programming of a public broadcaster; partly as the mother of two talented and wonderful professionals in their own right. And so on and so forth.

It may be hard to believe that as time has moved on, my own desire to stand on centre stage and think, "Wow this feels great!" has diminished considerably. I prefer to manage from behind the scenes and let others in the family be in the spotlight and applaud their performances.

Secondly, this has been a private matter between myself and my father. The letters I mean. He wrote them to me and at the time none of us probably ever thought they would get published.

So, is this the right thing to be doing is a question which has plagued me and continues to do. Am I breaking a sacred trust here? Am I guilty of some sort of a betrayal to perhaps the only person I am indebted to for so much in this life? Do I want to share these private moments with the world at large?

Will anybody actually understand the bond I shared (and still share) with my father? This is one side of him that no one (other than my sister) ever knew. Do I want to give even away and make it public?

Who do I look like the most?

Two peas – One pod Same gardeners – Different flowers!!

And hence the hesitation, the anxiety, the holding back, the delay, until it became a nagging thought.
And here I am, at the very beginning.
And it begins, a journey back through time.

A journey which will cause me (some) pain and heartache, as well as joy as I relive the past. A journey which will make me rethink relationships; a journey which will probably make me wish I had not taken it up but nonetheless a journey which may make me feel relieved to have taken it up; a journey in which I must ask for forgiveness and understanding (in advance) of all those who I may hurt, embarrass, scratch or irritate. That never was, or ever could be, my intention.
But it is a journey of love and a tribute to the one human being, who I know loved me unconditionally, hugged me, held my hand, gave me a smile in those times when I felt lost, alone and abandoned.

A person, who I too (in my own very limited way), have loved back unconditionally despite that time and again I wanted to have a confrontation with him, yell at him, fight with him, tell him off or forsake him. And who now, in the twilight of my life, I miss more than when he was actually present here with me.

And so, dear reader, I present to you, Faiz Ahmad Faiz, the father.

For the reader

Before you begin reading, I want to share with you how this book came about and why.
There are only two people in this entire world who knew Faiz the way we did, my sister and myself. That thought has kept bothering me and also, at the same time, made me feel very special. Throughout my life I have met so many diverse people from all over the world who have shared memories, comments, letters, "guftagoo" of Faiz with me, with varying levels of credibility. Often, I have smiled (that "I don't believe you" smile which does not touch the corners of your eyes but is really just an exercise of your face muscles) and heard all the anecdotes. When I have doubted the veracity of a story, I have nodded at appropriate moments and even looked surprised, interested, amazed (depending on the story I was being told and who was telling it) and hoping they believed the charade. But then who am I to tell and judge.

And all those times I have thought repeatedly to myself, "Why don't you tell your story? You knew him in ways no one else did. You loved him as no one did. You waited for him, watched out for him, cried for him, laughed with him, talked to him, read to him, wrote to him, received from him, held him, hugged him, cooked for him, served him, shared your inner heart with him like no one else did. So what's holding you back?"

And I took the decision (as I do all the important decisions of my life) in one moment, taking the plunge and just diving in. The saying, "Take a leap and the net shall appear" seems to fit so accurately to my style of reacting to situations which require decision making. And the net somehow does appear.

So, I announced at the Karachi Literature Festival four years ago that I was bringing into the public eye letters from my father, and surprisingly I kept up the refrain for four years. This was totally unlike me, as it is not typical of me to procrastinate to the extent I have done.

Why the hesitation?
If someone who is in the business of writing had asked me, "What did you just announce? Do you know what it is you actually committed out there on a public platform? Do you have any idea what or how you are going to achieve this task?" the answer would have been, no. No idea at all.

So how was this venture even going to begin? That's when I started thinking seriously about it.
I talked of and about this book ad nauseam for months and years, to friends, to writers, to mentors, to well-wishers, to family, to publishers. Each time I brought it up, the general response I received was, "Well, get on with it", along with advice as to how to go about it.

I heard the input. I let it wash over me and fill me with confidence and motivation. Then the next day or week I would let myself be bogged down with everyday humdrum chores and all the enthusiasm would dissipate.

During my early morning walks in parks all over the world, I would talk to the trees, writing copiously in my head. I recalled so much of what I wanted to put into this book. I smiled at some thoughts. I dug deeper into my mind to pull out a memory, a comment, a visual, all the time savouring the process.

Those many evenings, afternoons and all times of the day when I had a "heart to heart" with so many remarkable people and picked their brains on why I should share these letters, how I should go about putting them together and what shape this book should take, are to be cherished far more than the actual process itself.
And here is where the gratitude and deep appreciation must be recorded.
All of you who have helped me through this entire journey, with all its stops and starts (more of the former but probably for good reason) and I am indeed deeply indebted to all of you.

First and foremost, both my sons, Ali and Adeel.
Ali, to make me kick-start the project, actually translated two of my father's letters into English. I can think of no one else who could have done a better job. Adeel talked to me at length on how to approach the project. The overall presentation of the book was his idea.

Both their wives Mona and Samer (in order of seniority!) have been my lifelines throughout this tedious and challenging journey.

Dr Arfa Syeda, Rukhsana Zia, Nyla Daud, Zille Huma, Maisoon Aziz, and Rukhsana Zeb (my "band of brothers") bore my whining, complaining and fussing about the reasons for the delays on countless occasions. I thank them for their patience, affection, words of encouragement and for never once rolling their eyes to say, "Oh no not that tale again!"

Atul Tiwari, who heard me out patiently in his flat in Mumbai on that July morning, with the rain beating down mercilessly, flooding most of the city, and advised me in his chaste Lucknawi Urdu, gently and persuasively, "To (bloody) get on with it!"
Aisha Sarwari, who never once lost faith in my "wanting to write", and probably understood the reasons which kept me from putting pen to paper, and still continued gently and silently to propel me in the right direction.

But the three most important people I am deeply indebted to are Sumera Khalil and Uzma T. Haroon. I shall mention the third last.
Uzma, who I asked over a casual cup of coffee in the Islamabad Club if she would edit my book, and Uzma being Uzma (the epitome of politeness and sweetness) said yes without probably thinking how disorganized and complicated this book was going to turn out to be. I write as and when the 'muse' beckons me. I write freely, without boundaries, as my heart dictates at that moment. Worse still, I never go back to read what I have written. It probably is a ghastly fact to admit, but it's true. Uzma bore my repeated requests to read and re-read the same chapters, keep a track on what, I wrote and then her gentle prodding to keep me focussed. I can never thank her enough for her patience putting up with my vacillations without complaint.

And then there is Sumera Khalil. For these past many months she has maintained a cool demeanour, despite my tantrums and emotional swings. Quietly, she would turn me around and bring me back on course; arrange my many appointments with the photographer, designer and publisher; draw up lists upon lists of photographs and documents that had to be dug up from across the world, Kabul, Konya, Jerusalem, Damascus, Shimla, London, Amman, Mumbai, Delhi to name just a few. Print and reprint the chapters to proof read until she knew each page by heart. Her name should be on the cover, as co-author, since her contribution is stamped on every word in this book.

And then last but not the least there is Bushy. Bushy and I have been friends forever. We shared the same hostel in Kinnaird College, we shared the same friends, we shared the same subjects in BA, we shared the same secrets as all teenagers do, we shared many laughs, the loss of our parents, birth of our grandchildren and their pranks, and political discussions. The list is endless.

This book that you are reading now has been reviewed and edited painstakingly by Bushy, word for word, sentence by sentence. I am so indebted to her love and continuous faith in me. This one is for you, Bushy.

Yet many others, who must remain unnamed, would ask and again and yet again, "Kitaab kahan tak pohnchi?" (Where has the book got to?) to be greeted with silence and a sigh from my end. There is however one person I messaged when I began to write. The comment that came back, "Zabardast", made me feel that I can do this. I heaved a sigh of relief and began to type away.

Could you see me, then, as the 'dictator' you described in my birthday poem?

Random thoughts about the structure

How should this book be structured was a thought which kept recurring off and on and was also the major deterrent in my maintaining focus.

One idea was to just publish the letters. But then that would not fully bring forth intimate segments of Faiz's personality.

I read the letters over and over again, trying each time to get hold of a thread or catch a brainwave to actually make them interesting for the reader. How was I to make this exercise of reading random letters written to a daughter by a father 'readable'? My letters, written to him and referred to several times, were obviously lost somewhere but I could still piece together some of the issues I raised in his letters from memory. There had to be some reference point, apart from the letters themselves that should focus on how he reacted.

Today, as I see my own grandchildren complain or bicker about the same matters, I actually tell them off and call them 'spoilt' or 'selfish' and there I was doing exactly the same thing four decades ago and wanting a sympathetic word from a father living hundreds of miles away. At the time there was no direct access to a quick response. No text messages, no WhatsApp, no messenger. But the life line of a father solving the problem, was my hope. He was always there for me.

Then one day Adeel came up with an idea which began to churn in my head at odd hours of the day and night; sitting at airports waiting for delayed flights; driving on long dusty journeys across the deserts of Sindh; flying for countless hours across the world.

And it all started connecting and coming together.

He died in 1984. After that so much has happened in my personal and professional life which he never knew about. I travelled far and wide; I received acclaim and international awards; rose through the ranks in my career; the boys got married and had kids; I went on Haj and so much more. I wanted to share all this with him, but it was too late. He had left the world.

So how about I write him letters now, in the present, and tell him all that had happened and continues to happen in my life? How about each of his letters 'then' getting connected to my letters 'now'?

The more I thought about it the more Adeel's idea appealed to me.
And that is how this book came to be structured.

Letter adressed to Hameeda Hashmi

Dear Abbu,

I found this letter just recently looking through the Faiz Ghar files.
It's dated April 16th, 1967.

I always had a vague connection with the date April 15th as something to do with my marriage proposal. So maybe it was this letter of yours which was received by Ammi (as I called my future mother-in-law in the years to come) which must have stayed with me.

As I read through it several times, I tried to gauge what was going on in your mind when you received her letter proposing a union between Humair and myself. I often used to wonder what Ammi might have written in it. She was a stickler for doing things in the culturally traditional manner, which I learnt after my many years of association with her. I may not (in fact did not) agree with much of what she believed in, but the tradition of "asking for the hand" of a future daughter-in-law is just too correct to find fault with.

Years later, when I had to do the same (twice), I realized that despite the children being in agreement on choosing their own life partners, there was still a certain amount of anxiety which I underwent as I stepped into their respective future in-laws' homes and made my "pitch"!

What I simply loved about this letter is the fact that you would ask for Bebe ji's permission, or her blessings more likely. As if she would ever refuse you anything!
You know what this reflects. It's the values of those times or the times you grew up in, when all important decisions were referred to the elders for their approval. Was it to make them feel valued? Was it to put the onus of responsibility on them in case anything went wrong? Or was it to simply maintain tradition? Perhaps all of above.
I feel so deprived of not having had you to go to when I was in the same situation with Ali and Adeel's rishtas and ask if I was doing it correctly.

I have felt lost without you so many times when making decisions or in times of crises. Sometimes I have made the right decisions, and sometimes not. Sometimes I have received appreciation for them, sometimes pain, sometimes satisfaction and sometimes despair.

At the end of the day the decision was always mine, and so was the cross which I bore with as much dignity as I could muster.

When you said you would write to Bebe ji.
What did you say? How did you address her? Did you make a case in my defence? Did you praise your future son-in-law to elicit a favourable decision from her? How did she convey her approval to you?

We all know she could not write or read except the Quran. She also did not approve or agree to taking telephone calls. Mysteries of the past haunt me with more questions. But the approval was duly accorded and a date was set for my marriage.

I do remember telling Mama about my choice of a marriage partner and her very matter of fact reply, "When you are financially independent you can get married, not before".

This response made me angry, hurt, resentful, depressed, not for a moment thinking she could be right.

This meant waiting, obviously, because I was at the time fresh out of college with a simple BA degree which meant a lot more in those days, I may add, but nevertheless it was still a fresh degree.

Where and how do I go looking for a job, was my first thought. Today, I can say with hindsight that Mama was a woman who perhaps saw into my future and wanted her daughter to never be dependent. Despite myself, I am grateful to her.
I went in for PTV training, got an appointment letter a few months down the line, and was married in November of the same year.

But one very important family member was missing at my wedding. Bebeji, who was so crucial in this entire process, died in May of that year but after she had given her permission for my marriage.

I loved her as dearly as she did me. She put up with my childish pranks with patience and tolerance. I ragged her endlessly. She would laugh at my antics, admonish me gently to no avail, scold me (which made no dent in my behaviour) threaten to tell on me, (which I knew she would never actually do). She was simply too fond of me to carry out any of the above threats. And I sorely missed her on that day.

I remember your silence when you came to Lahore to bid her a final goodbye. You sat stoically in the drawing room, smoking and looking into the distance, detatched and aloof, trying to come to terms with having lost your mother.

She used to tell me you were a very good child, undemanding, patient, content with your lot. You never cried or threw tantrums like other children, never got into fights or arguments.

I remember your coming to see her, where both of you did not converse much. After the initial, "Ki haal hai?" type of conversation there would be a peaceful silence. You would smoke and she would chew her niswaar and rotate her fingers on her tasbeeh. After a while you would say, "Fair main chalna aan" (I will leave now), and she would nod her head. You would come forward and bend over, and she would bless you with her hand and that would be it. But the bond of love was strong. It was a strong commitment between both of you, an intimate relationship, wanting nothing, expecting nothing, demanding nothing.

And that is exactly why Ammi's letter had to be shared with her.

Letter

Haji Abdullah Haroon College
Shah Walliullah Road, Khadda, Karachi-2

16th April 1967

Dear Sister Hameeda
I sincerely regret the delay in responding to your letter. Actually I was intending to travel to Lahore and was thinking of talking to you in person but the program has had to be postponed. Perhaps it may be a couple of days before I can come.
Your request is, understandably, appreciated by us and the relationship between Humair and Moneeza will delight us. I only need my honourable mother's blessings for the decision. Please do go and see her one of these days. She is probably with Maryam Apa currently. You can ask Meezo for the address. I shall be writing to her myself also.

Alys and I are well and in good health and I hope you all are well and happy too.
We just received a card from Salima in Paris. She appears to be busy sightseeing.
With much regard,

Sincerely,
Yours' truly,
Faiz

With my grandmother Bebe Ji

خط

عزیزہ حمیدہ بہن، اسلام علیکم

مجھے افسوس ہے کہ آپ کے خط کا جواب لکھنے میں تاخیر ہوگئی۔ میں خود لاہور آ رہا تھا، خیال تھا زبانی بات ہوجائے گی، لیکن وہ پروگرام ملتوی کرنا پڑا۔ شائد چند دن کے بعد آنا ہو سکے۔

آپ کا پیغام ظاہر ہے ہمارے لئے قابلِ قبول ہے اور عزیزی حمیر اور منیزہ کی نسبت طے پا جانے سے ہمیں مسرت ہوگی۔ صرف والدہ صاحبہ کی اجازت مزید درکار ہے۔ آپ کسی دن فرصت کے وقت اُن سے مل آیئے۔ آج کل وہ غالباً سمن آباد میں آپا مریم کے ہاں ہیں۔ میزو سے پتہ دریافت کرلیجیئے۔ میں خود بھی اُنہیں لکھ رہا ہوں۔

ایلس اور میں بخیر و عافیت ہیں، اُمید ہے آپ سب لوگ بھی خوش و خرم ہوں گے۔ سلیمہ کا ابھی ابھی پیرس سے کارڈ آیا ہے، سیر میں مصروف ہیں۔

زیادہ پیار

فقط

مخلص

فیض

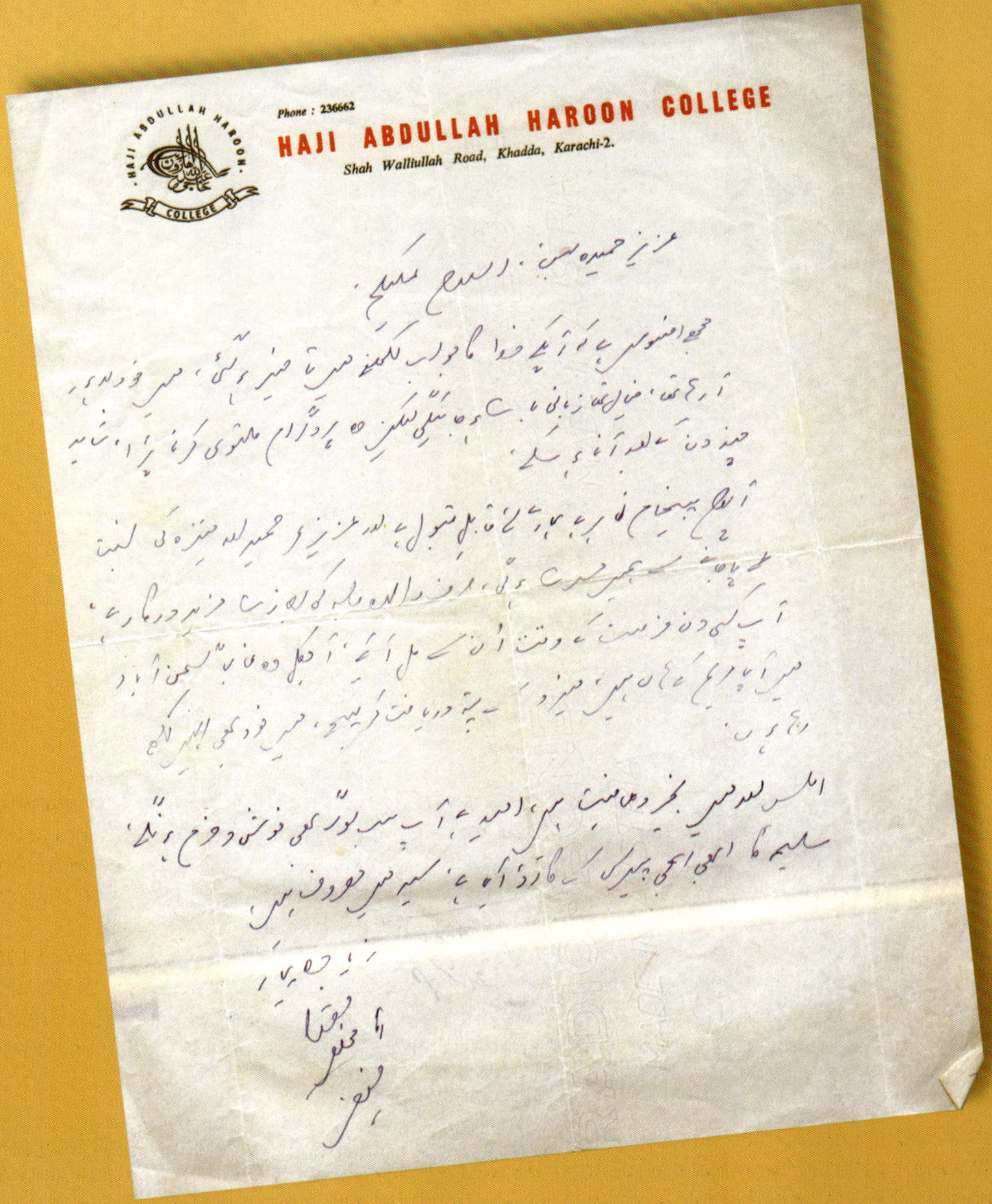

Phone : 236662

HAJI ABDULLAH HAROON COLLEGE

Shah Walliullah Road, Khadda, Karachi-2.

HAJI ABDULLAH HAROON COLLEGE

عزیز حمیدہ بہن۔ السلام علیکم

مجھے افسوس ہے کہ آپ کے خط کا جواب لکھنے میں تاخیر ہو گئی۔ میں خود دو دن
اور بیمار تھی۔ خیال تھا زبانی بات کروں گی لیکن وہ پروگرام ملتوی کرنا پڑا۔ شاید
چند دن کے بعد آنا ہو سکے۔

آپ کا پیغام نظر سے گزرا، ہمارے لئے قابل قبول ہے۔ البتہ عزیزی حمید اللہ چند دن کی مہلت
چاہتے ہیں۔ بہتر صورت یہ ہو گی، عرفان والدہ اور ماموں کو لے کر فریدہ کو دیکھ آئیں۔
آپ کسی دن فرصت کے وقت ان سے مل آئیں۔ آج کل وہ بہت مصروف ہیں۔
میرا پتہ ... ہیں، فیروز سے پتہ دریافت کر لیجیے۔ میں خود بھی ...
رہی ہوں۔

الحمد للہ میں بخیر و عافیت ہوں، امید ہے آپ سب لوگ بھی خوش و خرم ہوں گے۔
سلیمہ کا ابھی ابھی ہیڈ کلرک کا آرڈر آیا ہے، اسی میں مصروف ہیں۔

زیادہ حد ادب

فقط

آپ کی مخلص

[illegible]

Whenever I see this photograph

Faiz's first visit to see his eldest grandson Ali in Lahore

Whenever I see this photo, I can feel your heart bursting with joy at the sight of your first grandson, although I don't think I have even a single photo of you actually holding him! You always did seem to have a horrific scare on your face whenever a grandkid was yelling and creating a ruckus. That I do remember. Probably disturbed your inner peace and calm! But then Ali was the first "Ali Da Pehla Number" (Ali is the first).

I remember Mama telling me that when I started my labour pains that cold night in December of 1968, you were fast asleep, after having been sedated with flu meds. Anyway, it was in the middle of the night and she tried to wake you up or tried to "inform" you of our impending departure to the hospital. She said you sort of mumbled in your sleep, "How is he?" clearly indicating that you somehow had an inkling that your first grandchild would be a boy.

Later you would tell Ali, "Hamari taran ziada shareef mat banna. Nuqsan uthao gay" (Do not be a good person like me. You will suffer the consequences), because Ali was the quiet, silent, gentle giant and you felt that his "gentleness" would or might stand in his way or hinder him in his quest for in life.

Adeel on the other hand always took you to task. He confronted you, challenged you, made you laugh, won chess games from you.

I wish you could know my grandchildren. All five of them are so amazingly different.
Let me introduce you to them. They can be taxing, adorable, exasperating, loving. All rolled into one.

Take Hamzah for example, my eldest.
You would have liked his inquisitive nature. He has absolutely this insane desire to get it "right" with absolutely no room for error, meticulously methodical. Brilliant mind.
His younger brother Mahir is as poles apart from him as they come. Casual, a "don't care" about anything and anyone attitude; will only eat exactly as he has had it cooked for the past umpteen years and no amount of convincing or cajoling will work. It is exasperating and yet his eyes and smile will always melt your heart.

Their sister Alina, as beautiful as they come, with the George genes shining through her grey eyes. Focussed, intelligent, loving, and headstrong only when it comes to standing up for her rights or wishes. Otherwise, as soft and pliable as a feather.

These are Ali's.
Adeel's are another story.
The eldest Zainab was the first girl in the Hashmi family of "males" only.
I survived a life of so many years listening only to male oriented dinner conversations: kite flying; obnoxious Punjabi swear words flying across the table; loud yells when calling out to the domestic staff; cricket and more cricket ad nauseam. The female anatomy also came under consideration at odd times.

So, when Zainab Mahtab (how she hates that second name!) came into our lives, at last I saw redemption and was relieved. And she has not proved me wrong. Her tongue is as sharp as she is petite taking the latter genes from her mother.

She is talented and creative inheriting those genes from her mother again, who is an architect, and also from her older grandma (my sister), affectionately known as Cheemie Dadi.

She is as fastidious and picky as her father, and for me to have to suffer two such beings in one life time is certainly unfair!

Ahmer Aftaab Hashmi is the youngest of my brood. Smart, sharp, musical, nimble, fast on his feet and in his excuses for just about everything. Being the youngest, he has the need to prove himself differently so he must be everywhere and do everything and do it the best and be first to cross the finishing line. Again, his father shines through, always wanting to beat everyone at everything and win. I want to tell you a small tale about Adeel to illustrate his competitive spirit. We were all getting together for group and family photo many years ago when Suhail (Adeel's paternal uncle as you remember) was still alive and on his yearly winter visits to the family.

Groups were being organized according to family status for the photographs. Adeel was moving round and round restlessly. He was all of three or four years old: golden hair, grey shining eyes.
I watched him for a bit and inquired the reason for his apparent distress. "Hamari bari kab ayay gi (When will it be our turn)?" he asked. I told him that whenever the photographer was ready he would call us. "Magar who walay jeet jain gay" (But the others will win), he wailed while pointing to Shoaib's family. For him it was always about being first, being the best, being ahead of everyone.

It still is.

Postcards

To
Ali Hashmi
120-H, Model Town Lahore
From
Tunis
14-9

Dear Ali,
We are now in Tunis. It is a very small country but its history is very extensive and interesting. The Greeks, the Arabs, the Spaniards, the French all have left behind ancient buildings like this famous city of Carthage which was destroyed by the Romans. The country has made considerable progress after liberation from France. There are numerous upper end hotels and very splendid bungalows. We are putting up with a friend, Moeen, in one such bungalow. Am looking for presents for you.

Lots of love,
Nana

To
Ali Hashmi
120-H, Model Town Lahore
From
Paris, France
14-5

Dear Ali,
You did not write again after that one letter. I have heard that you have grown really tall but it is not good to grow too tall because they say that very tall men are fools.

Lots of love,
Nana

Father with Nana (grandfather)

Son with Dadi (grandmother)

To
Adeel Hashmi
From Russia

Dear Adeel,
How big are you now? Two feet or more than that and how much can you read beyond Alif Bay? And what about the naughtiness? I shall come to see you when you grow another two inches.

Lots of love,
Nana

To
Ali Madeeh Hashmi
From
Moscow, Russia

My dear Ali,
I sent a card to you all before this which you might have received. I am indulging here in a very big Moscow hospital. I have to go to the gymnasium early morning, after waking up. The patients go there in groups according to their ages and obviously the oldest make up my class.... sans teeth, sans guts, as they say! Then I ask myself whether I too am as old as them? Then I shut my eyes tightly so that I can't see all those old people. Next week shall be discharged.

Lots of love,
Nana

My family during COVID Eid 2020
L to R: Mavra Hashmi, Ali Madeeh Hashmi, Humair Hashmi, Myself, Mahir Ali Hashmi, Adeel Omer Hashmi, Samer Hashmi
Seated on floor, L to R: Zainab Mahtab Hashmi, Hamzah Ali Hashmi, Alina Ali Hashmi
Seated in front: Ahmer Aftab Hashmi

پوسٹ کارڈز

To
Ali Madih Hashmi
G-156 Model Town, Lahore
From
Tunis
14-9

پیارے علی

اب ہم تیونس پہنچ گئے ہیں۔ ملک تو بہت چھوٹا سا ہے لیکن اس کی تاریخ بہت لمبی اور دلچسپ ہے۔ یہاں یونانی، روسی، عرب، ہسپانوی، فرانسیسی سب پرانی عمارتیں چھوڑ گئے ہیں جیسے Carthage کا یہ مشہور شہر ہے۔ جِسے Romans نے تباہ کیا تھا۔ فرانس کے آزاد ہونے کے بعد ملک نے کافی ترقی کی ہے۔ بیشمار بڑھیا ہوٹل اور بت عمدہ بنگلے ہیں۔ ایسے ہی ایک بنگلے میں ہم اپنے دوست معین کے پاس ٹھہرے ہیں۔ تمہارے لئے تحفہ تلاش کر رہے ہیں۔

بہت سا پیار
نانا

To
Ali Hashmi
120-H, Model Town Lahore
From
Paris, France
14-5

پیارے علی

آپ نے ایک خط کے بعد پھر کوئی خط نہیں لکھا اور سنا ہے آپ کا قد بہت بڑھ گیا ہے۔ لیکن زیادہ لمبا نہیں ہونا چاہیئے۔ کہتے ہیں کہ زیادہ لمبے آدمی احمق ہوتے ہیں۔

بہت سا پیار
نانا

A happy carefree moment with Nana (grandfather) at 102 H, Model Town

To
Adeel Hashmi
From Russia

پیارے عدیل میاں

اب آپ کتنے بڑے ہو گئے ہیں، دو فُٹ یا اس سے زیادہ اور الف بے کے بعد کتنا پڑھ لیا ہے؟ شرارت کا کیا حال ہے؟ جب آپ دو انچ اور بڑے ہو جائیں گے تو ہم ملنے آئیں گے۔

بہت سا پیار
نانا

To
Ali Madeeh Hashmi
From
Moscow, Russia

پیارے علی جان

تم لوگوں کو ایک کارڈ پہلے بھیجا تھا، شاید مل گیا ہوگا۔ اب ہم ماسکو کے بہت بڑے ہسپتال میں کچھ عیاشی کر رہے ہیں۔ صبح اُٹھتے ہی ورزش کے لئے جمنیزیم جانا پڑتا ہے۔ سب مریض عمر کے حساب سے الگ الگ گروہ میں جاتے ہیں، ظاہر ہے کہ ہماری کلاس میں سب سے زیادہ بوڑھے شامل ہیں۔ نہ منہ میں سب دانت، نہ پیٹ میں آنت۔ اور ہم اپنے آپ سے پوچھتے ہیں، کیا ہم بھی اتنے بوڑھے ہیں؟ پھر ہم exercise آنکھیں بند کر کے کرتے ہیں تا کہ یہ بوڑھے نظر نہ آئیں۔ ہم کو اگلے ہفتے چھٹی مل جائے گی۔

بہت سا پیار
نانا

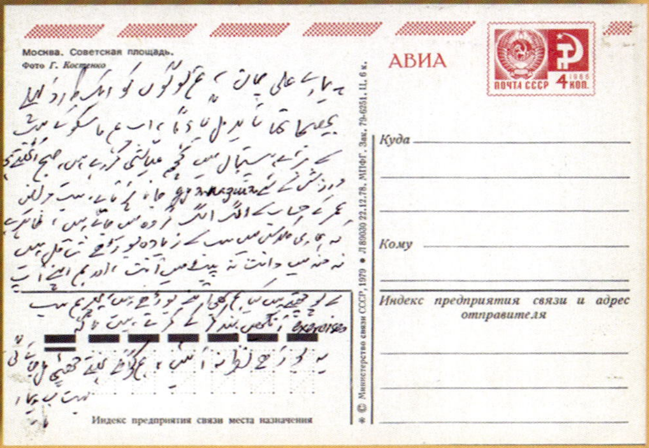
Москва. Советская площадь.
Фото Г. Костенко
АВИА
ПОЧТА СССР 4 КОП.
Куда
Кому
Индекс предприятия связи и адрес отправителя
Индекс предприятия связи места назначения

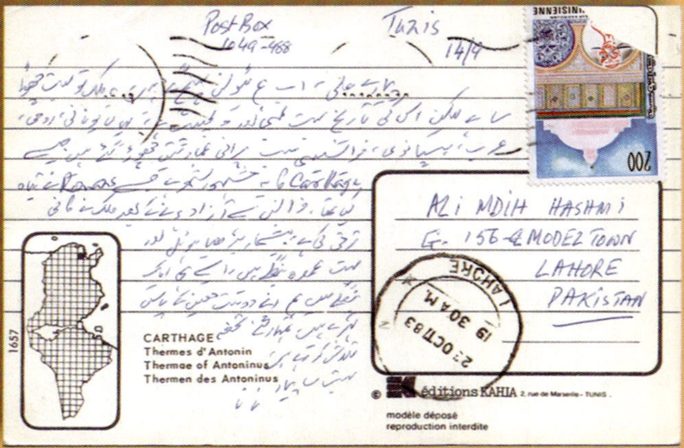
CARTHAGE
Thermes d'Antonin
Thermae of Antoninus
Thermen des Antoninus
1657
200
LAHORE
PAKISTAN
Éditions KAHIA 2, rue de Marseille - TUNIS
modèle déposé
reproduction interdite

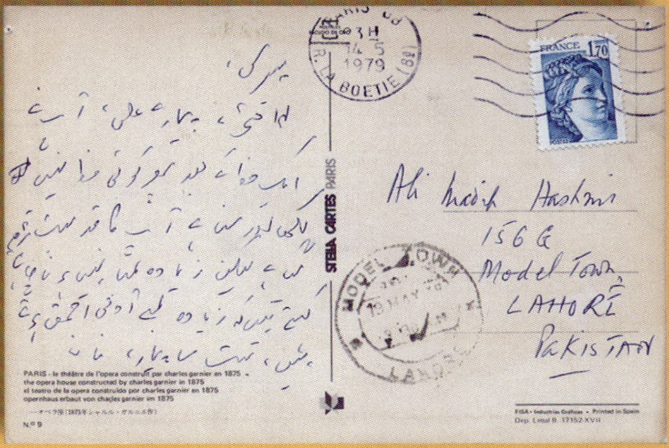
STELLA CARTES PARIS
FRANCE 1,70
Ali Malik Hashmi
156 G
Model Town
LAHORE
PAKISTAN
PARIS - le théâtre de l'opera construit par charles garnier en 1875
the opera house constructed by charles garnier in 1875
el teatro de la opera construido por charles garnier en 1875
opernhaus erbaut von chajles garnier im 1875
N.º 9
FISA - Industrias Gráficas - Printed in Spain
Dep. Legal B. 17152-XVII

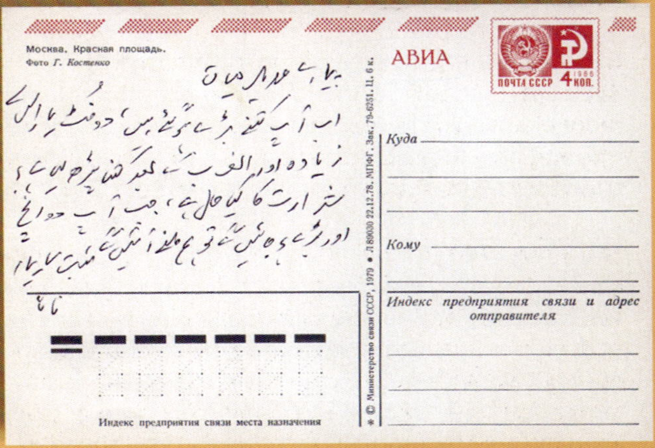
Москва. Красная площадь.
Фото Г. Костенко
АВИА
ПОЧТА СССР 4 КОП.
Куда
Кому
Индекс предприятия связи и адрес отправителя
Индекс предприятия связи места назначения

Asking for money

I'm not sure how or when or why I "saved" this learning in my hard drive, that I must not ask for money or borrow money from anyone. And if I do, I must return it as soon as I am able to.

I never really had more than I needed at any particular time. I was never wanting but I was never flush either, always having just enough to get by. And somehow whenever a dire need appeared, so did the opportunity to fulfil it with my own resources. I think that is probably what you had to face throughout your life.

I found out much later, from how many different ways or different avenues you would receive money to keep our needs satisfied.

I never ever remember Mama and yourself having a discussion about money. There was always food on the table, our school and college fees were paid, we had clothes in the cupboard, even though it was second hand stuff from Landa Bazaar (flea market) as I remember buying sweaters from the pavement outside Mayo Hospital, but we were warm in the winter and protected from the sun in the summer. There were no luxuries, that's true, but I suppose that taught us to value fancy food and other luxury articles when we did come across them: the ice creams, the rides in cars, the movies and treats in the intervals, the birthday presents under our beds, the Eid jaunts to collect precious eidi which bought us chaat and channas in school, my first watch that Bhai Saeed gave me for my birthday, the year he died. I could go on and on.

As I was saying, I just have never been able to ask anyone for money, no matter how dire the need.

And yet the only person who I did ask was you. Never once did I feel embarrassed or ashamed asking you for cash or other favours. You and I had that relationship of absolute trust, self-esteem and immense love. In college I was always cribbing about the heat, bad food, cold water in the freezing winter. You always had your wallet open, quietly doling out to my needs. When we were building our house, I remember the $500 gift (that built Ali's bedroom and bathroom), which you slid into my hand with a smile and a wink, more of a twinkle in your eye. And we always hid this from Mama, who kept mentioning how you spoilt me, and how important it was for us to learn to "do without". You mention this so openly in your letter. "Don't tell Mama," you wrote. It was a sort of conspiracy between you and me.

You knew I was struggling to make ends meet, bringing up my two boys, working in a job that was both challenging and rewarding but at the same time made me feel threatened and despondent. You knew I was frustrated and at times almost clinging to sanity to carry on. You knew I was not cut out to take orders or decisions against the strict code of ethics and integrity instilled in me, and you also knew that I was no quitter. I would face up to the challenges of intolerance, gender discrimination and prejudice against my family. You knew that I would depend on an inner strength that would make me push harder, strive more, keep my eyes focused on the ultimate goal. You knew I would come out bruised, but not defeated. And the funny part, now as I reflect is, that I knew you knew. I knew you were probably the only person in the

The thought of you gave me the courage to withstand ridicule and misogynistic remarks hurled at me from all sides.

I remember the cold morning of 14th December, 1958 when a black car came to fetch me from school. As I reached home, I watched you walk away, accompanied by strange men who had come to arrest you a day after you arrived home from London. I felt the physical blow of losing you again. You never looked back and did not see my expression of, "Where are you going Abu? When will you be back?" The pain of losing you without explanation will always remain with me.
I still can't ask anyone for money, because it was only you with whom I had that connection.

Believe it or not your support still keeps coming to me. Money from the royalties of your poems. Money that seems to appear at the most unusual and yet most appropriate times.

I see a concerned father watching out for me.

Letters

001/64
Abdullah Haroon Secondary School
Shah Walliullah Road, Khadda, Karachi-2

1 / 10
Dear Moneeza,
My affections.
I hope you are safe and sound. The money that you asked for is being sent. This should do for you till the next month. Your mother is feeling a bit unwell and says that she will be writing to you in two or three days, but it is nothing to worry about ... just a slight cold. The luggage has still not arrived but is probably expected today and then your things shall be sent to you.
Love to everybody.
Your Abbu

To: Moneeza Faiz
2nd Year Student
Kinnaird College Hostel, Kinnaird College
Gulberg Road, Lahore

001 / 66

Mizu my dear,
Lots of love.
First, I received your letter which worried me but then your telephone call relieved me. You should have stayed with us for some more days. Lahore's heat and the hostel food would not have appeared so bad. My daughter there are times when the weather, a bout of ill health, or the distance from loved ones can pull anybody down but then this mood always passes away. Last night I dreamt of you and you looked happy and beautiful. I hope the dream would have become a reality by now.

If you don't like hostel food, then get something for yourself from the market. Don't be thinking of money like your mother. You can draw some money from your bank account or send for some from me. Rest assured, your mother will not mind it. If you want to come here in the vacations instead of going somewhere else then by all means, do come. Even if we are not here, both Khadija and Ratna who both miss you, will be glad to have you here.
There is nothing definite about our departure as yet, but we will decide in a couple of days and let you know. You just take care of your health my love. There is no need to worry over anything. Of course, there is no panacea to the heat but surely it too will pass in a few days. Then in any case next year by summer we will all be together. Either you will be in Karachi or we will be in Lahore so there is no reason to worry.

Affections to Hameeda, Shoaib and Humair.
Yours,
Abbu

002 /66
Haji Abdullah Haroon College
Shah Walliullah Road, Khadda, Karachi-2

9 /6 /1966
Dear Mizu,
Love!
I called you twice the day before yesterday, but you were not available. Regret at not being able to talk to you because I wanted to find out about your programme. Now you write to me and let me know if you need anything. Next Sunday I shall again try to talk to you. If instead of Mason Road you can come to Nageen at Majeed Uncle's house on Sunday, it will be good because usually there is always a call from there on Sundays. In any case you must write to me. Lots of love.

Yours,
Abbu

001 /68
Haji Abdullah Haroon College
Shah Walliullah Road, Khadda, Karachi-2

Dear Mizu,
Love.
Here, take your money! For the delay in returning the loan I have increased the interest!
I hope Humair dearest will have regained his health and you are all well. Affections to Hameeda Begum.

Yours,
Abbu

خطوط

001/64
Abdullah Haroon Secondary School
Shah Walliullah Road, Khadda, Karachi-2

۱/۱۰

پیاری میزو

پیار

امید ہے تم خیروعافیت سے ہوگی، پیسے جو تم نے مانگے تھے بھیجے جا رہے ہیں۔ اگلے مہینے تک تمہارے لئے کافی ہونگے۔ امی کی طبیعت کچھ خراب ہے اس لئے انہوں نے کہا ہے کہ وہ دو تین دن کے بعد تمہیں خط لکھیں گی۔ ویسے کوئی فکر کی بات نہیں زکام وغیرہ ہے۔ سامان ابھی گھر نہیں پہنچا، غالباً آج آجائے گا، پھر تمہاری چیزیں بھجوادی جائیں گی۔

سب لوگوں کو پیار

فقط

ابو

To
Moneeza Faiz
2nd Year Student
Kinnaird College Hostel, Kinnaird College
Gulberg Road, Lahore

001/66

پیاری میزو جان

بہت سا پیار

پہلے تمہارا خط ملا جس سے بہت پریشانی ہوئی، پھر تمہارے ٹیلیفون سے کچھ اطمینان ہوا۔ تمہیں ابھی کچھ دن اور ہمارے پاس رہنا چاہیئے تھا۔ تمہاری طبیعت بالکل ٹھیک ہو جاتی تو شاید لاہور کی گرمی اور ہوسٹل کا کھانا اتنا برا نہ لگتا۔ ویسے کبھی کبھی تو بیٹی موسم کی خرابی، یا طبیعت کی ناسازی یا عزیزوں کی دوری سے ہر کسی کا جی گھبراتا ہے لیکن پھر یہ موڈ گزر بھی جاتا ہے، کل رات تمہیں خواب میں دیکھا تھا اور تم خوش اور خوبصورت نظر آ رہی تھیں۔ امید ہے اب تک خواب سچا ثابت ہو چکا ہوگا۔

اگر تمہیں ہوسٹل کا کھانا پسند نہیں ہے تو باہر سے کچھ منگوالیا کرو۔ اپنی اماں کی طرح پیسوں کے بارے میں مت سوچا کرو۔ اول تو اپنے بینک سے نکلوالیا کرو یا ہم سے منگوالیا کرو۔ امی کچھ نہیں کہیں گی۔ چھٹیوں میں اگر کسی اور جگہ کی بجائے یہاں آنے کو جی چاہتا ہے تو ضرور آ جاؤ۔ ہم نہیں بھی ہوئے تو خدیجہ اور رتنا دونوں ہیں جو تمہیں بہت یاد کرتے ہیں اور تمہارے آنے سے خوش ہونگے۔

ہمارے جانے کا ابھی ٹھیک سے طے نہیں ہوا، دو چار دن تک فیصلہ کرینگے۔ پھر تمہیں لکھ دیں گے، تم صرف اپنی صحت کا خیال رکھو جان اور کسی بات پر پریشان ہونے کی ضرورت نہیں ہے۔ گرمی کا تو خیر کوئی علاج نہیں لیکن اب تھوڑے دنوں میں وہ بھی گزر جائینگی۔ پھر اگلے سال گرمیوں کے آنے تک تو بہر صورت ہم اکٹھے ہونگے یا تم کراچی میں یا ہم لاہور میں، اس لئے کچھ فکر کی بات نہیں۔

حمیدہ، شعیب اور حمیر کو پیار۔

فقط

ابو

002 /66
Haji Abdullah Haroon College
Shah Walliullah Road, Khadda, Karachi-2

9 /6 /1966

پیاری میزو پیار،

پرسوں تمہیں دو دفعہ ٹیلیفون کیا لیکن تم دونوں دفعہ غیر حاضر تھیں۔ افسوس ہے بات نہ ہو سکی، تمہارے پروگرام کا پوچھنا تھا۔ اب مجھے خط میں لکھ دو اور کسی چیز کی ضرورت ہو تو وہ بھی بتا دینا۔ آئندہ اتوار کو پھر تم سے بات کرنے کی کوشش کروں گا۔ اگر تم اتوار کی صبح کو میسن روڈ کے بجائے مجید چچا کے ہاں نگین کے پاس آسکو تو بہت اچھا ہو اس لئے وہاں سے ایک ٹیلیفون بہر حال اتوار کو یہاں آتا ہے۔ بہر صورت جیسے بھی ہو مجھے خط ضرور لکھ دینا۔ بہت سا پیار۔

فقط

ابو

001 /68
Haji Abdullah Haroon College
Shah Walliullah Road, Khadda, Karachi-2

پیاری میزو

پیار

لو بھئی اپنے پیسے۔ واپس کرنے میں دیر ہو گئی۔ اس لئے سود بڑھا دیا ہے۔

امید ہے عزیزی حمیرا اب صحت یاب ہو چکے ہونگے۔ اور تم سب بخیر و عافیت ہو گے۔ حمیدہ بیگم کو پیار۔

فقط

ابو

Actual Letters

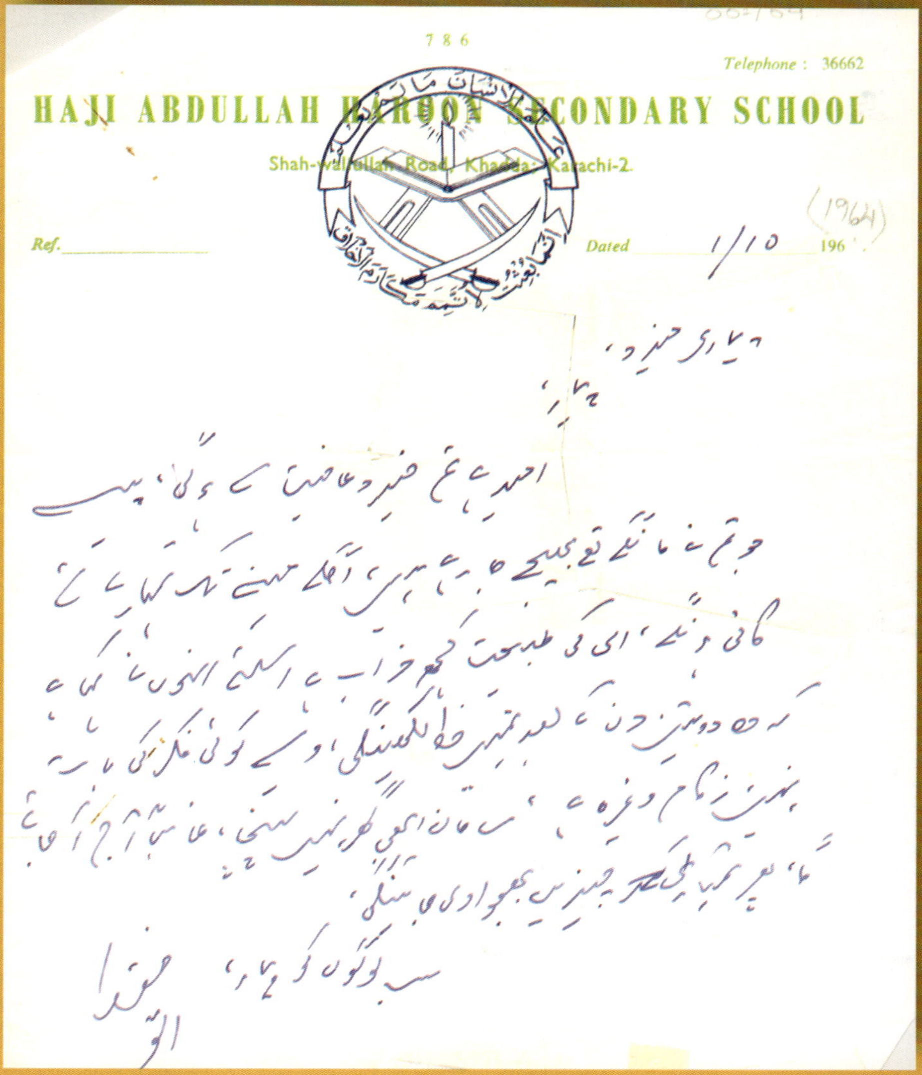

786

Telephone : 36662

HAJI ABDULLAH HAROON SECONDARY SCHOOL

Shah-waliullah Road, Khadda, Karachi-2.

Ref.______________ Dated 1/10 196 (1964)

ڈیئر حمیدہ،

پیار،

الحمدللہ تم خیر و عافیت سے ہو گی، پیسے
جو تم نے مانگے تھے بھیجے جا رہے ہیں۔ اگلے مہینے تک تمہارے ابا آ جائیں
گے، امی کی طبیعت کچھ خراب ہے اسلئے انہوں نے کہا ہے
کہ وہ دو تین دن کے بعد تمہیں خط لکھیں گی، اور سے کوئی فکر کی بات
نہیں، کام وغیرہ ہے؟ سب کام ابھی تک نہیں ہوئے، ... آج ...
تو پھر تمہارا ... چیزیں بھجوا دی جائیں گی۔

سب لوگوں کو پیار،

تمہارا
ابو

Actual Letters

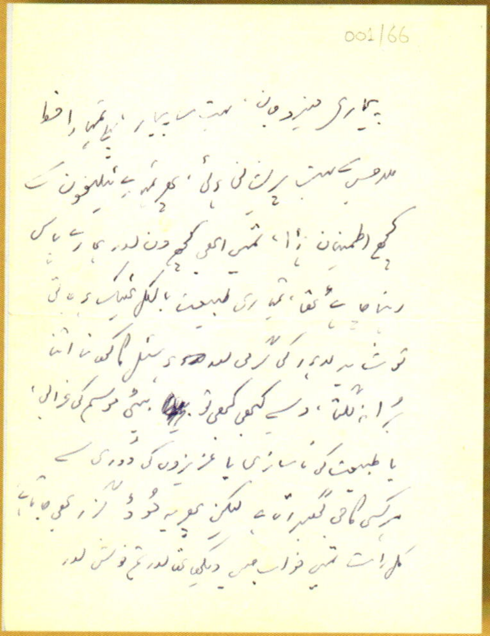

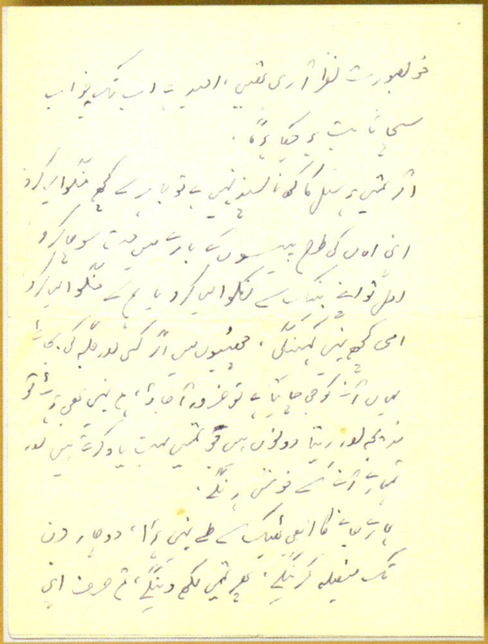

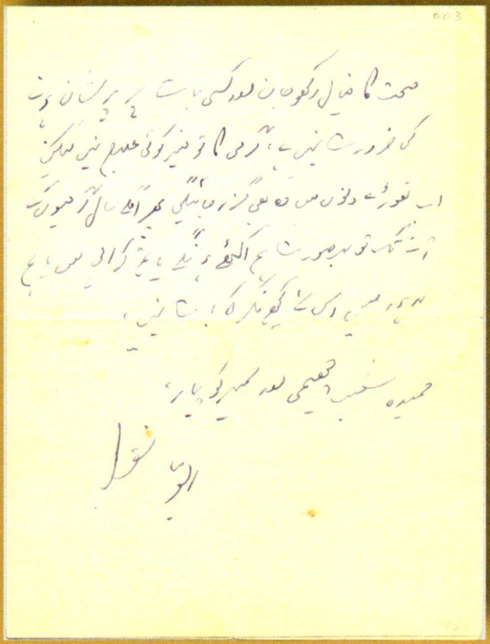

002/66

786

Telephone : 36662

HAJI ABDULLAH HAROON COLLEGE

KHADDA, KARACHI-2.

Ref.________ Dated 9/6 196 .

پیاری حمیدہ، پیاری،

پچھلے ہفتے دو دفعہ ٹیلیفون کیا لیکن تم دونوں دفعہ غیر حاضر
تھیں۔ افسوس ہے بات نہ ہو سکی۔ تمہارے پروگرام کا کچھ علم
نہیں۔ اب مجھے خواہش لکھ دو کہ کسی چیز کی ضرورت ہو
تو وہ بھی بتا دینا۔ آئندہ اتوار کو پھر تم سے بات کرنے کی
کوشش کروں گا۔ اگر تم اتوار کی صبح کوشش کرو تو بہتر ہے
حمید جب آئے [illegible] ٹیلیفون کے پاس آ سکو تو بہت اچھا ہو [illegible]
[illegible] ایک ٹیلیفون بہرحال اتوار کو ہو جائے۔ بہرحال
جیسے بھی ہو مجھے خط ضرور لکھ دینا۔ بہت بہت پیار
فقط
ابو

001/68

Phone : 225098

HAJI ABDULLAH HAROON COLLEGE

Shah Walliullah Road, Khadda, Karachi-2.

پیاری حمیدہ،

خط ملا۔

دو کتابیں دے رہا ہوں۔ واپسی کی [illegible]
سود [illegible] دیا ہے۔
[illegible] عزیزی حمید اب [illegible] ہو گئے ہیں۔ الحمد
سب بخیر و عافیت ہیں۔ حمیدہ بیٹی کو پیار۔

فقط
ابو

So what are the most vivid memories I have of you

So what are the most vivid memories I have of you, or should I say why or when do I remember you most vividly?

To begin with, when I see Ali and Adeel interacting with their daughters, talking to them, pampering them, submitting to their every whim and wish, helping them with their homework, taking them out wherever they demand, are proud of their achievements, plan for their future in terms of vision and finances or simply listen to them natter and chatter on and on, however meaningless it may seem at the time. That is when I miss you most.

I never had moments of sharing such joys with you.
You were never around. And when you were, there were so many others who laid more claim to your time than I.

Now listen up. This is not a complaint box re-opened after three or more decades of your passing. It is simply the wailing of a daughter who misses you now more than she did when she was younger. Frankly I was involved in so much going on in my life back then.

School, then College, then PTV, then marriage, then kids, then University. And so on and so forth.

But what was missing throughout was your presence.
And now, in the twilight of my life, I realize how much of that vacuum exists within me.
And what am I doing about it?

I obviously am being convinced to smile at the camera

I am filling it by sharing with my grandchildren with as many memories and stories and experiences as I can. So that when they grow to a ripe old age, they can tell their kids all the funny stories I told them about their dads and myself. Isn't that the best way of passing on the baton?

Yet there are strong and vibrant memories of the times when I did manage to sneak in some time with you.

My days in Kinnaird College were wonderful, where I made friends for life, and who, even today stand by me are my strength and share a laugh with me. But let's face it, I was miserable on several accounts in the hostel then and I must have moaned about it to you then because your letters at the time are so gentle and warm.

It has always been hot in Lahore and was especially so to a 17-year-old lying on a manji (sitting bed) under the stars, trying to sleep, with mosquitoes buzzing in her face, dorm mates chattering and a very early sunrise flashing on heavy eye lids. Your letters telling me to be patient were probably not what I wanted to hear at the time, but today seem so similar to what I am preaching to my brood, as they complain of load shedding and flies and more of the same. My 'forever' lack of funds is also so lovingly addressed by you. You would send me "extra" pocket money saying not to tell Mama. We both knew how she would react. Firstly to your spoiling me, as she called it, and secondly to your taking over control of a domain she claimed as her own, the girls and their upbringing. And today, my "famous five" can literally walk all over me when it comes to 'financing' anything they want, with their mothers voicing their opposition at my 'extravagance' and I am sure their reasons are probably very much in line with Mama's!

There were opportunities (very few and far between, unfortunately) when you did visit Lahore and took me out for a meal, usually lunch, and saved me from the hostel, at times inedible food.

With you came whiffs of Pacco Romma after shave and cigarette smoke. 555 was the tin that I associated with you or 3 Castles. Tweed coats, if I still see them anywhere, bring back in my mind's eye your bear-like figure. Wooden buttons on jackets are another favourite image of mine, as well as silk dressing gowns and open black slippers, 'arraha' pyjamas and straight starched mulmul (thin cotton) kurtas (there was no lawn at the time if I am correct). A favourite of yours was Burgundy pump shoes. You slept on your side with both hands in fists curled under your cheek. You did snore, I remember, as I could hear you clearly once in a while when I was outside your room. You were an early riser, no matter what time you had slept the night before. Your intrepid travelling made you quite the Vasco de Gama of my time. Once, when on one of those late night coaches to Karachi on a three-hour flight I went into my usual palpitations as the plane began to jerk and shake, you calmly told me to imagine I was on a bumpy road with stops and starts, and the car engine was trying to find a smoother path. It worked that time and has since, on all my hundreds of journeys across many continents. You, at the time, simply put a pillow under your head and promptly went off to sleep.
You would do that even when the bombardment in Beirut was at its worst. 'Switch off' your letter tells me. When you can't do anything about it, switch off. What reasonable and sane advice. That must have been how you kept your sanity intact all those years in jail, and in exile, and when you were faced with critics, or when you faced personal and other losses, and when you were trying to find a meaning to the insanity prevailing in Pakistan in the Zia era, and when you were followed, harassed, phone tapped and discriminated against.

There could be no better way to actually punish your opponents and critics and enemies.
Switch off. I do not see you. I do not hear you. You cannot hurt me. You are not a part of my world.

I have done that on so many occasions when I was being targeted in PTV during the Zia era and beyond. My fault was, of course, that I was Faiz's daughter. How idiotic is that, I would think. But I soon found out that by switching off and simply ignoring them, I was causing them more frustration and pain than if I had fought a full-fledged battle. I would only get my nose bloodied and they would get a broken jaw. But the score would still not be settled.

However, this way they would be barking up a one-way street and would ultimately get tired and leave. And that is exactly how it happened. Years later, when erstwhile enemies became "buddies", I would smirk and think, "Oh yeah?"

There is so much I want to tell you about my PTV days. After all forty years or more is half a life time. I had my ups and downs, probably more of the latter, but now, today, am I still there in the ring throwing a few punches at my opponents? Well, some are gone and the ones still around are, shall we say 'spent' forces. Yes, it has been quite an innings in PTV.

But more of that in another letter.

KC, Class of '67, horsing around – literally!!

Class of 1967 – Sports Day, Kinnaird College, Lahore

KC Najmuddin Dramatic Society production "Ring Around the Moon" 1966
Who is the handsome guy seated on the left side of the photograph!

Letter

002 /79
Beirut, Lebanon
June 4

Dear Mizu,
I received your letter after many days. It made me happy.
Your Summer School thing is good but I don't understand the need to go around looking for words. This job can easily be done from the house with help from library books but there is no harm in some free entertainment. Khatir Ghaznavi, Farigh Bukhari and other friends are there in Peshawar. In Quetta you could run into either Major Muhammad Afzal (who was with me in the army at one time), former minister Gul Khan Naseer or my childhood friend Muhammad Nawaz, a well-known lawyer. If your leave ends on June 15th how will you manage to do all this work?
It is good that the plans of the shop have been drawn up but people usually start construction work after December or January when the rains stop and days become longer. Still, you people know better.
I enjoyed Adeel's remark. That rumour about the Nobel Prize, whoever started it is a job well done. Who do you think is going to give me the prize…but the gossip feels good. I have told Cheemi my programme; first the hospital, then London, then America, London again and inshallah back home by October.

Love to Humair, Ali and Adeel.
Abbu

خط

پیاری میزو
بہت دنوں کے بعد تمہارا خط ملا، خوشی ہوئی۔
تمہارا Summer School تو ٹھیک ہے لیکن الفاظ ڈھونڈنے کے لئے ادھر ادھر جانا ہماری سمجھ میں نہیں آیا۔ یہ کام تو گھر میں بیٹھ کر لائبریری کی کتابوں سے بھی ہوسکتا ہے لیکن مفت کی سیر میں کیا ہرج ہے۔ پشاور میں خاطر غزنوی، فارغ بخاری اور دوسرے دوست موجود ہیں۔ کوئٹہ میں میجر محمد افضل جو کسی زمانے میں فوج میں ہمارے ساتھ تھے، سابق وزیر گل خان نصیر، اور ایک ہمارے بچپن کے دوست محمد نواز مشہور وکیل ہیں، شاید ان میں سے کوئی تمہیں مل جائے۔ اگر تمہاری چھٹی ۱۵ جون کو ختم ہو رہی ہے تو یہ سب کام کیسے کرو گی۔
دکان کا نقشہ بن گیا ہے تو اچھی بات ہے ویسے عام طور سے لوگ تعمیر کا کام دسمبر جنوری کے بعد شروع کرتے ہیں جب بارش رک جائے اور دن لمبے ہو جائیں، لیکن آپ لوگ بہتر جانتے ہیں۔
عدیل کی بات کا بہت لطف آیا، نوبل پرائز کی ہوائی جس کسی نے بھی اڑائی ہے بہت اچھا کیا ہے۔ پرائز تو ہمیں کون دے گا لیکن اشتہاری ہی سہی۔ چھیمی کو اپنا پروگرام بتا دیا ہے، پہلے ہسپتال، پھر لندن، پھر امریکہ، پھر لندن، پھر انشا اللہ اکتوبر تک واپس گھر۔
حمیر، علی اور عدیل کو بہت سا پیار
ابو

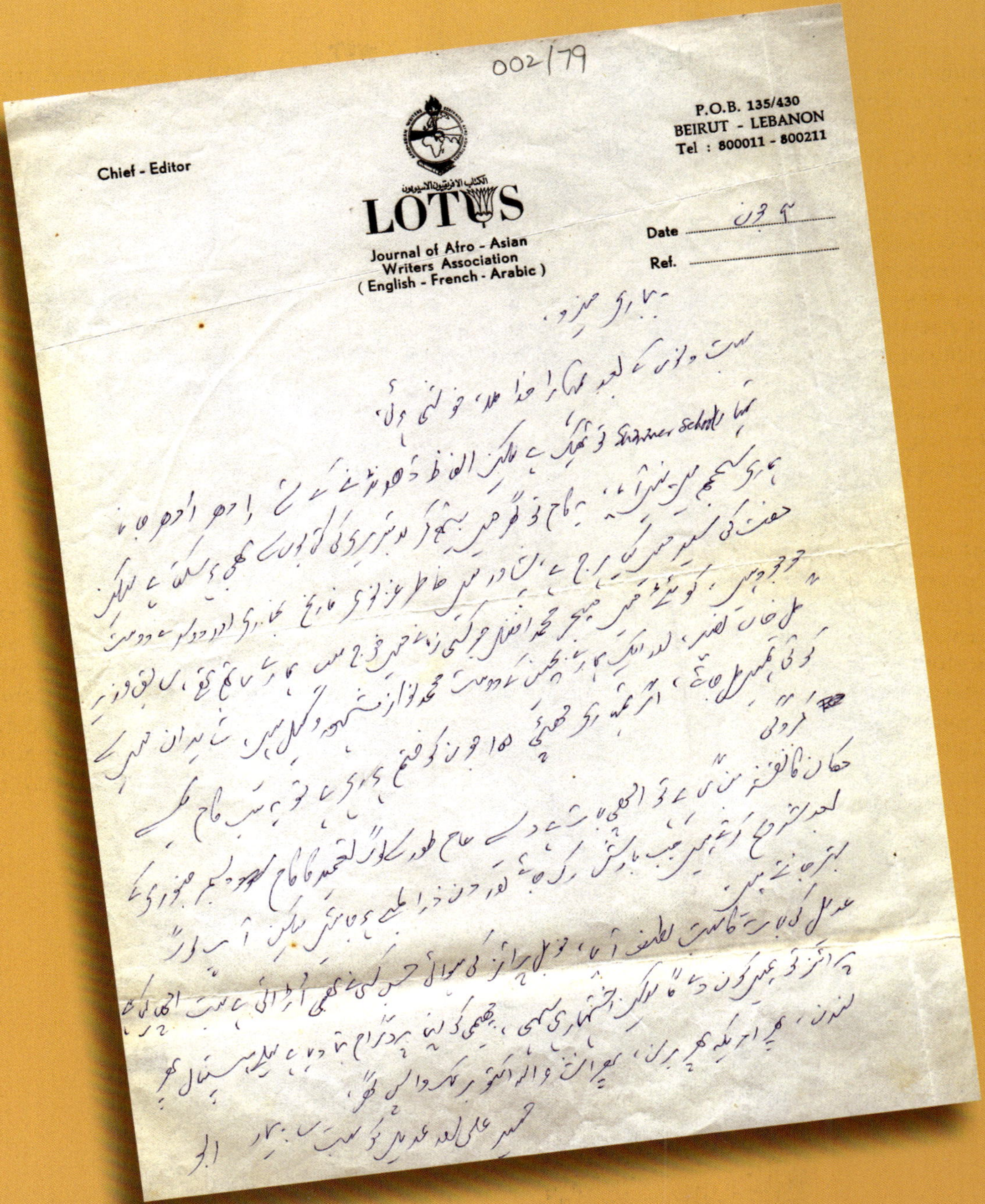
002/79

Chief - Editor

الکتاب الافریقیون الاسیویون

LOTUS

Journal of Afro - Asian
Writers Association
(English - French - Arabic)

P.O.B. 135/430
BEIRUT - LEBANON
Tel : 800011 - 800211

Date ۳ جون

Ref.

پیارے حمید،

بہت دنوں کے بعد تمہارا خط ملا، خوشی ہوئی۔

تمہارا Summer School تو ٹھیک ہے لیکن الفاظ ڈھونڈنے کے لئے

ہماری سمجھ میں نہیں آتا۔ یہاں تو گھر میں بیٹھ کر دشمنوں کی گولیوں سے بھی بچ سکتے ہیں لیکن ادھر ادھر جا کر

حفاظت کی [illegible] ہے۔ اس دوران میں خاطر غزنوی، فارغ بخاری اور دو ایک دوست

جو ہم سے [illegible] محمد افضل [illegible]

[illegible] دوست محمد نواز [illegible]

[illegible]

جہاں [illegible] ۱۵ جون کو ختم ہو رہی ہے تو [illegible]

[illegible]

[illegible]

[illegible]

لندن، پھر امریکہ [illegible] واپس [illegible]

حمید، علی اور عدیل کو بہت بہت پیار

[illegible]

Smugness thy name is Faiz

I clearly remember that one time when we were walking down Oxford Street in London and someone stopped and greeted you and wished you good health. You smiled, shook hands, said thank you and we walked on.
I asked you, "Who was that?"

"I don't know," you said as we walked on.
"But you greeted him as if you knew him!" I exclaimed.
You smiled mischievously. "Bhaee he knew me. I guess that's all that counted for him!!"
I have never forgotten that incident even though it took place decades ago. Somehow I got the feeling then that you did enjoy the fame and recognition and glamour that went into being "the" Faiz. Partly, your humility was to smooth over that feeling of smugness or satisfaction of knowing exactly how brilliant you were. I think all of us at one point or the other in our lives (some more than others) are aware of how well we did something, said something, thought of something, wrote something, sang something, cooked something, painted something and the list can go on and on.
And yet a word of praise (although we may crave it) can embarrass or lessen that inner sense of satisfaction.

There were many other times when I would see people fawning over you at social gatherings, recognizing you in markets, stopping you in conferences simply to have a word with you, shake your hand, say something, anything, have a paper signed as an autograph to take home, and so on. I know from personal experience how tiresome these encounters can be, to have total strangers walk up to you and demand your attention in your face, I know you did enjoy it somewhat. Of course, let's not forget there were less people on this planet back then, and the curse of the mobile phone with instant selfies was nowhere on the horizon. So it was not such a huge irritation as it is now to be accosted and a "pic with you" literally begged for. But I think you did enjoy the recognition once in a while. Just read that letter in which you talk about the students who recognized you in the far away beach of Sandspit, and when they heard it was your birthday, then of course it turned into a party, with you as the centre of attraction.

I do know you were generally a shy and retiring sort of person. You did not like to bring undue notice to yourself or any "good" deeds you did for anyone. How often have I been accosted here and there by people who have told me of the time when you would make a phone call on their behalf to someone, for a job or a transfer or a loan from a bank. Not only that, you would go that extra mile to visit or call upon the person who needed to be contacted. Much to their embarrassment, you would walk into the office of a junior officer in some nondescript office, sit down with the person, have a cup of tea and leave after signing an autograph for the officer in charge. Hopefully the file would have gotten approved later simply because you had recommended it. People have a habit of saying "abhi karta hoon Sir" (I will just do it), and the poor person still has to make countless visits to the office to finally make the file move.

I recall once way back in the Zia ul Haq days, when my file came up for approval to a short trip for Germany as a PTV representative. I had followed the file through to get the required NOC, and my visa had been stamped in advance and the ticket purchased.

A female bureaucrat (no names to be taken as she is still around, though probably very old now) said to my face, "But this does not have the signature of so and so", or something equally irrelevant. The person she mentioned was the Secretary of Information at the time, Mr Nasim Ahmad, who was obviously way out of my reach. "But Madam, I have a flight later today," I told her, almost in tears. That did not move her and I left her office mentally calculating my next move, as I stumbled along the corridors of power in the Secretariat in Islamabad. I made my way to the office of Secretary Information. As my good luck would have it he was in his office. I took a deep breath and asked to see him. "Aap kaun hain?" (Who are you?) asked the mini-god sitting outside called his PS

"Faiz Ahmed Faiz ki beti," (daughter of Faiz Ahmed Faiz) I said. I was called in. You were praised by Mr Ahmed who was both courteous and polite. I got the file signed. I went back to Madam's office, only to find that she had left the office with instructions that if I should come back I should be given the NOC! So what was the fuss all about still escapes me, except to show me who was the boss! Exactly why am I telling you this now after so many years? Well, I guess simply to share with you some of those not-so-nice memories that just stay with you and don't go away. And also how your name got me out of that mess. You must have had a pretty big bunch of those types in your time. It's all very easy to say "move on", but you know, there are scratches that still sometimes ooze a bit, a pinch here or there which makes you wince, an itch that won't go away and constantly burns. Stuff like that.

Ever so often I run into someone who now would like to be my best friend, whilst a few years ago they would not have told me the time of day if I had asked. Someone who suddenly recalls "those wonderful moments we shared", and I can't for the life of me even recall having met them, let alone shared 'moments' with them. Then there are others who insist that when I was General Manager I had done this or said that. I have to put on that idiotic smile, which even my grandchildren, if they are around, comment on later, "And Dadi (grandmother) just looked at that person wishing them to dissolve into thin air but she was smiling! How do you do that Dadi?" they ask. "A lot of practice my dear," I tell them.

Yeah. Growing old and facing the twilight as it approaches is not just difficult, it's terrifying. But you know what? Just knowing that I will not be there to see these children start their own lives as adults is what makes me feel so sad. Having seen them change from toddlers to walkers, to runners, to dancers, to computer geniuses, to argumentative teenagers, to cinema companions, to critics of my hair and makeup, to advisors treating bruises on my body, to handling my social media hassles, to cracking jokes, to holding my hand as I struggle up stairs, to heating my food or rubbing cream on my back, etc., etc. Yes I will miss them, just as much as I miss you....

Letter

001 /65
Sandspit, Karachi
Sunday
February 13th

Dear Mizu darling,
I am writing from Sandspit and today is Sunday the thirteenth of February, which, I just remembered, perhaps happens to be my birthday! The recall, because nobody reminded me of it.

We were to spend the day here with the artist Sadequain. So I got up in the morning to call a lot of people in the hope that somebody would be ready to accompany us but nobody was ready to commit. In the end Ammee and I got here by ourselves. I had assumed that Sadequain would be all by himself so I would be able to read and write while he painted. But what do we see when we arrived … an entire army of policemen from one end to the other. The emperor's own cavalcade was to pass by. When we got to the hut there was this huge bus parked alongside it and inside there was this throng of girls, girls, girls filling every available inch of space. Sadequain explained apologetically that they were medical students who had arrived unannounced and hoped that we would not mind. So, I said all right, the more the merrier. O God! what a cacophony ...Thin, fat, tall, short, fair skinned, dark skinned, blue, yellow, all sizes and colours, no idea how many of them. Somebody in the crowd recognized me and then a full-throated mantra aka Naara-i-Hyderi was raised for autographs. What followed was an hour or so of hard labour and since nobody had a diary or paper, half of your mother's writing pad fell prey. Now, after having eaten they are playing rock 'n roll records which makes me want to write to you.

It is pleasant today after many days and Ammee and I are sitting out in the sun (inside another army has taken over) but the sun is not bothering us. There is a slight chill in the breeze and warmth in the sun, as in Lahore in the spring.

Your college classes must have commenced. Here, every college except Khadda is closed. Anyway, I have not been too disturbed by this confusion in the colleges because first you and then Cheemi came along. Now I have to think up of an excuse to get your colleges to shut down so that you may visit again otherwise it is going to be quite a while before we meet.

Lots of love,
Abbu

خط

001 /65
Sandspit, Karachi
Sunday
February 13th

پیاری میزو جانم

ہم Sandspit سے بول رہے ہیں، آج اتوار کا دن ہے اور فروری کی تیرہ تاریخ، جو ابھی یاد آیا کہ شاید ہماری سالگرہ کا دن ہے، اس لئے کہ اور کسی نے یاد نہیں دلایا۔ تو آج ہمارا مصور صادقین کے یہاں دن گزارنے کا وعدہ تھا۔ صبح اٹھ کر بہت سے لوگوں کو ٹیلیفون کیا کہ کوئی ساتھی چلنے کو آمادہ ہو جائے لیکن کسی نے ہامی نہ بھری، آخر میں میں اور امی اکیلے یہاں پہنچے۔ خیال تھا کہ صادقین کے علاوہ اور تو کوئی ہو گا نہیں وہ بیٹھ کر تصویریں بنائیں گے ہم پڑھنے لکھنے کا کام کریں گے۔ خیر قریب آئے تو کیا دیکھتے ہیں کہ یہاں سے وہاں تک پولیس کھڑی ہے۔ پتہ چلا کہ بادشاہ کی سواری گزر رہی ہے، پھر ہٹ (hut) میں پہنچے تو سامنے ایک بہت بڑی سی بس (bus) کھڑی تھی اور ہٹ کے اندر فرش سے عرش تک لڑکیاں ہی لڑکیاں بھری ہیں۔ صادقین نے معذرت کرتے ہوئے کہا کہ یہ میڈیکل کالج کی بچیاں بغیر اطلاع کے آ گئی تھیں۔ امید ہے آپ برا نہ مانیں گے، ہم نے کہا کہ ٹھیک ہے رونق ہے، افوہ! کوئی ہڑ بونگ ہے۔ پتلی، موٹی، لمبی، چھوٹی، سفید، کالی، نیلی، پیلی، ہر سائز اور رنگ کی نہ جانے کتنی لڑکیاں ہیں۔ بیچ میں سے کسی نے ہمیں پہچان لیا اور آٹو گراف کے لئے نعرہ حیدری بلند کیا۔ پھر کیا تھا آدھ پون گھنٹہ اس مشقت میں صرف ہوا اور کسی کے پاس ڈائری اور کاغذ تو تھا نہیں اس لئے امی کا آدھا پیڈ (pad) ان کی نذر ہو گیا۔ اب یہ لوگ کھا پی کر (Rock'n Roll) کے ریکارڈ بجا رہی ہیں جس پر تم کو خط لکھنے کو جی چاہا۔ آج بہت دنوں کے بعد موسم اچھا ہے۔ میں اور امی باہر دھوپ میں بیٹھے ہیں (اندر hut پر تو دوسری فوج کا قبضہ ہے) لیکن دھوپ بالکل بری نہیں لگتی۔ ہوا میں ہلکی ہلکی ٹھنڈک اور دھوپ میں ہلکی ہلکی گرمی ہے جیسے لاہور میں بہار کے موسم میں ہوتی ہے۔

تمہارا کالج تو کھل گیا ہو گا، یہاں پر کھڈہ کے علاوہ باقی سب کالج ابھی بند ہیں۔ خیر ہم تو اس کالجوں کی گڑ بڑ سے کچھ ناخوش نہیں ہیں اس لئے کہ پہلے تم آ گئیں، پھر چھیمی آ گئی۔ اب سوچنا پڑیگا کہ کس بہانے سے پھر تمہارے کالج بند کروائیں تا کہ تم پھر آ جاؤ۔ ورنہ تو بہت دنوں کے بعد ملاقات ہو گی۔

اچھا خط لمبا ہو گیا۔ باقی پھر لکھیں گے۔

بہت سا پیار

ابو

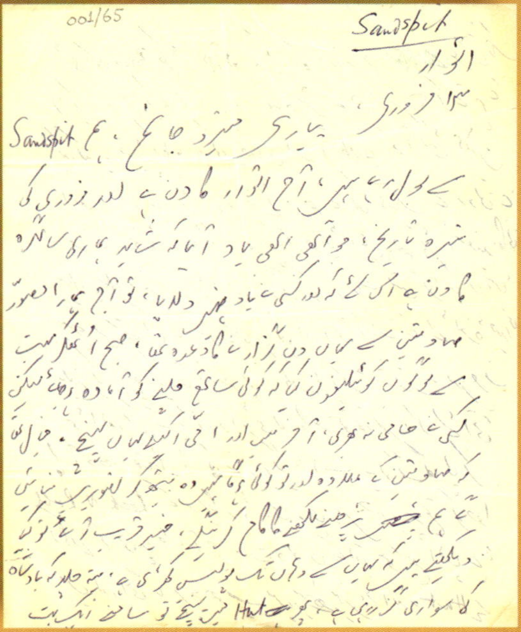

001/65

Sandspit

اتوار

۱۳ فروری

Sandspit ۶۰ پیاری منیزہ جانو،

سے لکھ رہی ہوں۔ آج اتوار کا دن ہے اور فروری کی
تیرہ تاریخ، جو ابھی ابھی یاد آیا کہ شاید ہماری سالگرہ
کا دن ہے اگر کسی نے یاد نہیں دلایا، تو آج ہم [illegible]
مہادوشن کے ساتھ دن گزارنے کا وعدہ تھا، صبح اٹھ کر بہت
سے لوگوں کو ٹیلیفون کیا کہ کوئی ساتھ چلنے کو آمادہ ہو لیکن
کسی نے حامی نہ بھری، آخر میں اور امی اکیلے یہاں پہنچے۔ [illegible]
کہ مہادوشن کے علاوہ اور کوئی آیا نہیں وہ بیٹھ کر [illegible]
[illegible] بیٹھ کے لکھنے کا کام کر رہی ہوں، خیر قریب آئے تو [illegible]
دیکھتے ہیں کہ یہاں سے دور تک پولیس کھڑی ہے [illegible]
کی سواری کر رہی ہے، پھر Hut میں پہنچے تو سامنے ایک [illegible]

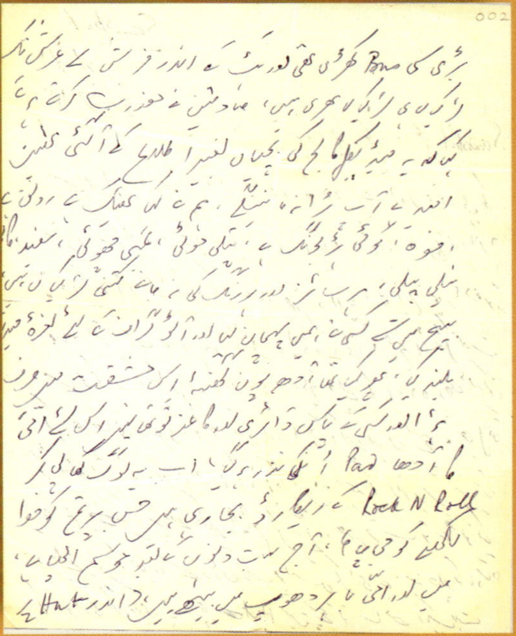

002

[illegible] Pond کھڑی تھی [illegible] کے اندر فرش کے [illegible]
[illegible] تھی ہیں، مہادوشن نے [illegible]
[illegible] کی بچیاں بغیر اطلاع کے آگئی تھیں
[illegible] سے آگے [illegible] نہ سکے، ہم نے ان کو کھانے کی [illegible]
[illegible] ہنسی خوشی [illegible]
[illegible]
[illegible]
[illegible] ایک مشقت [illegible]
[illegible]
[illegible] Pad [illegible]
[illegible] Rock N Roll [illegible]
[illegible] آج بہت دنوں کے بعد [illegible]
[illegible] دھوپ میں بیٹھی ہیں، اندر Hut کے

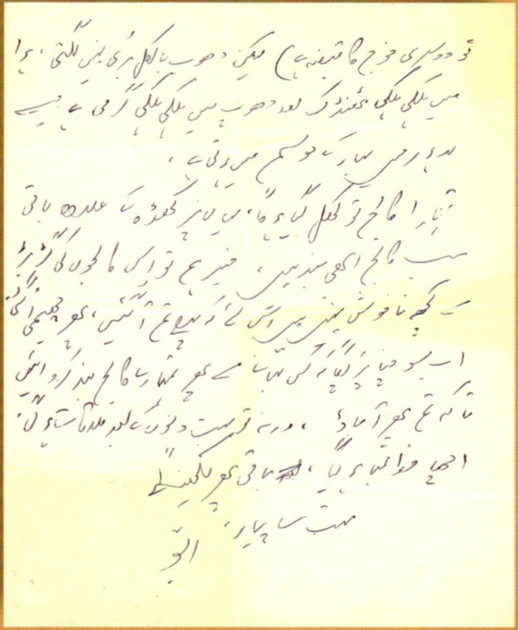

تو دوسری طرح کا شغل ہے) لیکن دھوپ بالکل بری نہیں لگتی، ہوا
میں ہلکی ہلکی ٹھنڈک اور دھوپ میں ہلکی ہلکی گرمی ہے جیسے
بہار میں ہمارے موسم میں ہوتی ہے۔
تمہارا کالج تو کھل گیا ہوگا، یہاں پر [illegible] کے علاوہ باقی
سب کالج ابھی بند ہیں، خیر یہ تو ایک [illegible]
سے کچھ ناخوش نہیں ہیں [illegible] آئیں گی، پھر [illegible]
[illegible] تمہارا کالج بند ہو [illegible]
[illegible] پھر آ جاؤ [illegible] بہت دنوں کے بعد [illegible]
اچھا خدا حافظ [illegible] باقی پھر لکھوں گی
بہت سا پیار،
امی

My birth certificate

I never really found out how you reacted to the fact that yet another daughter had been born to you in Shimla on August 22nd, 1946. How and when did you receive that news, who brought it and how were you informed is still a mystery to me.

Shimla, Himachal Pradesh. Locked away in the mountains of North India was where I entered the world. There are two incidents related to Shimla that I need to tell you about.

Out of the blue, an acquaintance a few years ago informed me that he was going with a group to Shimla for a conference.

Visas to India, as we all know, are almost as impossible to procure as it would be to become Chief Minister of Punjab. For me at least.

My eyes widened. I took a sharp breath and said: "Waqar, can I ask you a favour?"
Upon his affirmation (again totally unprepared and for apparent reason) I said, "Do you think you can get my birth certificate from Shimla?"

He agreed to explore and that was the end of it. Or so I thought.
I received a call on my cell a few days later from an unknown number. It was Waqar. "Where exactly were you born?" He wanted the name of the hospital or clinic. I had no clue obviously and was at a loss, as all the elders who would have known had passed on without indulging this information. And anyway why would I want to know I thought. Then suddenly, a brainwave.

Salman (Salman Taseer – maternal cousin) was a year older than myself. He was born just a year earlier in July, in Shimla. Maybe both the sisters had visited the same hospital; Mama and Aunty Chris (Christable Taseer - Alys Faiz's elder sister)
A call to Salma, Salman's elder sister, divulged the name of his birth hospital. It was conveyed to the contact in Shimla, but with the reservation that it was only a possibility, not a confirmation.

Two days later a call came through again, from Shimla. The information I had given was correct. We had both been born in the same clinic. Records had been searched in many sheds, where mice were roaming freely, but my birth details had not been chewed into tatters, and two weeks later I received the certificate and a kind letter from the Chief Minister of Himachal inviting me to Shimla someday.

Arriving in Shimla by train 2015

The nursing home where I was born is now Clarkes Hotel, Shimla 2015

I held that paper in my hand and went back 60 odd years.

The year was 1946.
Partition was being talked about but apparently not too imminent. Hence the certificate was never applied for. But then the countries were divided; families were torn apart, houses abandoned, borders defined and closed. It took more than sixty years or more for me to become legitimized, I thought to myself, as I kept looking at the certificate. Why was it so important for me to obtain it? I wondered. Why did I feel so fulfilled as I read it again and again?

That would all come home to me a few years later when I would apply for a British passport and would need "proof" of my birth. That paper would be worth its weight in gold for me.

But do you know, something else quite ridiculous happened. I put away the certificate so "safely" that I could not find it when the time came for me to complete my documents for application for my British citizenship! I looked high and low, went in and out of cupboards, over threw drawers, went quite berserk and into depression, but no result.
I called up my contact in Delhi once again. Sheepishly I asked for a second copy. "We don't do second copies in India," he told me, somewhat surprised at my request. "Sajjad, I need it desperately. Please can you go to Shimla again?"

There are times when the Heavens are aligned and all signs and all prayers are being processed in your favour. This was one such occasion. He did go back. He did get a second copy made. He did send it over to me and, in fact, he sent two copies. "One for you to submit and one for you to misplace again," he said. The pun was not lost on me.
Just for the record I found the original a few months later. But by then my British papers were done, my application approved, my oath to Her Majesty administered and my red passport in my drawer (again) but this time where I can see it every time I open it.

The second story is about my own visit to Shimla.
I have to tell you this because we never did discuss anything about my childhood or actually anything about your past. I hear parents sharing so many memories about their childhood with their children. I do the same with all five of my grandkids. I find it so relaxing and such fun to share silly escapades or tell them stories about their fathers. They lap them up and then go running to their dads to tell them what they know. And of course the boys find out they could only have gotten it from one undeniable source. The grandkids love hearing about how their dads, who appear so knowledgeable and strict, were actually quite the opposite in their childhood. But I never had this kind of opportunity with either you or Mama. I have some scattered memories of my own and some from Aunty Bali (Faiz's younger half-sister), but other than that I draw a blank page as I try to draw on my memories when I was a baby and learning to eat, walk, talk or early school and so much more.

But I digress from the Shimla story which is where I was headed. There are many stories there too, but let me stay on course here for the moment.

Shimla had been with me, it would seem, forever. I had wanted to visit it for no reason except to see where I was born, but no opportunity seemed to be forthcoming. It was not accessible by a flight perhaps and that could be one reason. There was a train journey involved and then a road trip and it just seemed too intimidating to arrange and plan, especially being in another country. Not so foreign, but still no doubt across the border. I heard of other people going and coming back and wished I had known in time to have joined those groups. I did at one time work it all out on my own but chickened out for no reason except simple nerves. But then it happened. Just like that. A net appeared and I took the leap.

I have often landed up in so many different places. Just like that. May be on a whim, an idea, a simple conversation, an urgent thought.

Siem Reap, Jaisalmer, Bethlehem, Sun City, Venice, Khujrao, Al Aqsa, Lake District, small villages in Wales, Buckingham Palace, Fiji, Srinagar, and many more.

Shimla was a result of one such conversation at a crowded cocktail party in Islamabad with an old and dear friend, Susan Wellsby. She happened to mention she was travelling to Shimla with her family. I happened to have a valid Indian visa at the time and that weekend free, and I happened to be in "that frame" of mind and Bob's your uncle.
Two weeks later I was in Susan's apartment in Delhi, getting to know her family. Early next morning we were on the train, and a few hours later we were packed into a mini-van and winding our way through Himachal's hills towards Shimla. The road reminded me so much of the road to Murree from Islamabad. Winding. Pine trees. Wind rustling through the trees. Trucks honking. Kids selling flowers enroute. It was so similar, and yet a world apart.

As we got out of the mini-van I was reminded again of Sunny Bank, Murree. I walked up to my small hotel off the main road and checked in. It had a tiny balcony overlooking the valley. I still could not believe I had actually made it to Shimla.
After a nap, I ambled up to the hotel where Susan and her family were staying. We then walked to the main meeting place where we mingled with hundreds of other tourists and walked around. We went for a longish walk on the road below which was the exact replica of the Mall Road in Murree. I kept twirling around trying to figure out each shop. Had it not been for the Hindi written on the main boards outside the shops, I could have been in Murree. And then guess what? One shop floored me completely. Hopson, it said. Chinese shoe makers. Surely I was dreaming, I thought. Susan thought I had gone a bit cuckoo when I stopped dead and said, "I don't believe it." "What?" she asked. Without answering her, I pushed open the door. She followed me. The smell of fresh leather, the beautifully placed shoes on racks, the rows and rows of "my kind" of shoes.

Was I dreaming? I expected Mr Kingson to pop out and greet me. Do you remember him? Surely you must. Such a decent chap.

"Can I help you?" asked a Chinese face.

"Just looking," I said, but then without missing a heartbeat I had to ask. "Are you Mr Hopson?" "My grandfather," he said. And then it came tumbling out: my childhood memories; the shops on the Mall in Lahore and Mr Kingson and his arch rival Hopson next door. We talked some more, before I realized Susan was feeling fidgety. I promised I would come back and left feeling warm and sad at the same time. How does one let go of one's childhood.

We kept walking, looking for the clinic where I was born. Not that I expected to find it after six score years, but I had to know. For closure at least. On we went, asking shopkeepers who looked us up and down. We were an odd couple, a foreigner and another semi-foreigner who spoke fluent Hindustani, as they call Urdu. We finally hit the target, only to find that it had been turned into a gorgeous hotel. I took a photograph outside the main board. I looked at it one more time and then it was time for lunch. The next day we walked up to the Residency, which is as beautiful as they come. The walk up was a killer, but the first sight of that magnificent building was worth the breathlessness and panting. Like all colonial buildings, it is a superb example of British Raj architecture, replete with its aura. Inside, the rooms are lined with teak panelling. The windows overlook the aesthetically laid out gardens. The furniture is so "Downton Abbey". It is awesome and overpowering. We wandered around in the lawns outside imagining tea parties with ladies and their parasols decked out in their Sunday best. Bearers serving cucumber sandwiches and cakes to gentlemen in top coats and watches on chains. It was straight out of the Colonial Era. The next day as a special celebration of my upcoming birthday, Susan had arranged for us to have high tea in a special boutique hotel. When the owner found out who I was and after the usual eye rolling, he informed me of some obscure contact with you which I swallowed gracefully (I hope) and we continued our visit. That house was totally unbelievable in as much as it was like stepping back into the 1920s. The furniture, the photographs on the walls, the armoury displayed everywhere, the carpets on the floor, the smell of the place was as if I was emerging out of layers and layers of linen. It was flowery and spicey. The bathrooms were simply straight out of Victoria and Abdul. The actual sink and tub had flowers engraved on them! I could just see Judy Dench step out of the bath and ask me, "Would you mind handing me my towel please?". The winding staircase was solid teak we were told. And then came the tea!

The bearers who served us were dressed in sparkling white uniforms with turbans (but of course); the cutlery was silver (but of course); the china was pure Dresden (but of course); the sandwiches were cucumber and cut paper thin (but of course); the cake was delicate and small (but of course); the tea was weak and a bit cold (but of course) and then came the best part. Craig, Susan's husband, had brought a bottle of champagne from Delhi which was popped and drunk with "Happy birthday" sung loud and clear! It was the most unforgettable birthday celebrated in April but as Susan said, "We have to celebrate it in Shimla".

The trip back to Delhi on the train was another adventure worth describing. We rode through102 tunnels. Chugging up and around mountains was a glorious experience. Can you imagine riding a train all around Murree and the Gallis with all that greenery, birds, clear blue skies, stations enroute (that again are so archaic and charming), simple mountain folk waving, kids selling flowers and nuts as we lumber on into yet another tunnel and out the other side into brilliant sunshine. The mountain air was crisp and clean. The trees were healthy and green. The birds sounded cheerful and happy. Breath taking. Captivating.

I wish I had asked Mama about her trip when she went up to "deliver" me in 1946.
How was it then? I would have liked to have a reference context to compare it to my experience. But back then I could never have imagined that I would ever make it to Shimla.
I did miss out here big time and will always regret it.
But Shimla. You have a special place in my heart now that I have connected with you after fifty nine years!

ASIAN AGE 6 AUG. 2007.

Pak poet's daughter gets Himachal gift

SPOTLIGHT

Shimla, Aug. 5: The daughter of famous Pakistani poet Faiz Ahmad Faiz has received an emotional gift from Himachal Pradesh chief minister Virbhadra Singh in the form of her birth certificate from Shimla Municipal Corporation.

Faiz's daughter Moneeza Hashmi, a journalist, was born in Shimla on August 22, 1946 when her parents visited the picturesque capital of the state.

Due to her sentimental attachment to the place of her birth, Ms Hashmi contacted the joint secretary of the Indian chapter of the South Asia Free Media Association, Mr Sajid Mirza, to obtain birth certificate during the forum's two-day convention here in the first week of June, Mr Mirza said.

He said he took her request to the chief minister, who took a personal interest in the matter and directed officials of the Shimla Municipal Corporation to trace the certificate.

The corporation's officials found her birth certificate after scouring through old records.

"The chief minister gave me the birth certificate for delivering it to her as a gift from him on her birthday later in August," Mr Mirza said.

Mr Mirza said he sent the certificate to Ms Moneeza Hashmi by courier last week. *(PTI)*

Outside the Viceroy Lodge, Shimla 2015

प्रपत्र संख्या-5
FORM No.-5

हिमाचल प्रदेश सरकार
GOVERNMENT OF HIMACHAL PRADESH
स्वास्थ्य एवं परिवार कल्याण विभाग
DEPARTMENT OF HEALTH & FAMILY WELFARE

हिमाचल प्रदेश

No.

जन्म प्रमाण-पत्र
BIRTH CERTIFICATE

(जन्म मृत्यु रजिस्ट्रीकरण अधिनियम, 1969 की धारा 12/17 तथा हिमाचल प्रदेश जन्म मृत्यु
(Issued under Section 12/17 of the Registration of Births and Deaths Act, 1969 and
रजिस्ट्रीकरण नियम, 2003 के नियम 8 के अन्तर्गत जारी किया गया)
Rule 8 of the Himachal Pradesh Registration of Births and Deaths Rules 2003)

यह प्रमाणित किया जाता है कि निम्नलिखित सूचना जन्म के मूल लेख से ली गई है जो कि (स्थानीय क्षेत्र) M.C. Shimla This is to certify that the following information has been taken from the original record of births which is the register for local area/local body) M.C. Shimla
तहसील (Tehsil) Shimla जिला (District) Shimla के रजिस्टर में उल्लिखित है।
Registered in the Register ——— of State/~~Union Territory~~ H.P

नाम/Name : ——— ———
लिंग/Sex Female

जन्म-तिथि/Date of Birth 22/8/46
जन्म-स्थान/Place of Birth 47, Marina Annexe Simla.

पिता का नाम/Name of Father Lt. Col. Faiz Ahmed Faiz

माता का नाम /Name of Mother ——— ———

माता पिता का स्थाई पता/Permanent address of the Parents

/ / /

पंजीकरण संख्या/Registration No. : 567/46
पंजीकरण दिनांक/Date of Registration 23/8/46.
दिनांक/Date of Issue : 10/7/07

Sub - Registrar
Births & Deaths
Municipal Corporation
Shimla - 171001
9/7/07

प्राधिकारी के हस्ताक्षर/
Signature of the Issuing authority

प्राधिकारी का पता/Address of the Issuing Authority

मोहर/Seal

राजकीय मुद्रणालय, हि0 प्र0, शिमला–2001–स्वास्थ्य/2004–25–9–2004–5,000.

VIRBHADRA SINGH
CHIEF MINISTER

हिमाचल प्रदेश

ELLERSLIE
SHIMLA-171 002

D.O.PS/CM-2007
Dated: July 18, 2007.

Dear Ms. Moneeza (Gul) Faiz,

I had received your request through SAFMA in India for your Birth Certificate from Municipal Corporation Shimla. I am enclosing the same in original along with photostat copies.

with regards.

Yours sincerely,

(Virbhadra Singh)

Ms Moneeza(Gul) Faiz,
C/o SAFMA,
Pakistan.

Do you also write poetry?

I cannot recall the number of times I have been asked this question. My response would vary depending on my mood at the time, or the person who was asking this rather silly question (in my opinion anyway), and maybe the weather or general ambience around us, etc.

I recall how many times you were also faced with equally silly questions. Like "Faiz Sahib when will all of this get better?" "Faiz Sahib will this ever get better?" "Faiz Sahib who will make this better?" Nobody ever asked what can we or I do to make it better. It was always someone else who had to put whatever was wrong right. And in this country there is so much wrong to be put right, all the time, every day, 24/7. And your answer would also depend on the three variables mentioned above. I wonder what you were thinking at the time.

Over the years, my responses changed from being apologetic (what a useless daughter I am to not write poetry), to a simple shake of the head and a smile (to tell the person to get out of my face), to a blank expression which sort of said "Me? Do you think I can write poetry?"

But do you know that on another note I never actually thought of you as "the" poet. To me you were Abu. Calm, sweet smelling, twinkling eyes, very tidily dressed always, (no matter how late you might have slept the night before), early riser, morning cup of tea with a newspaper kind of person.

Faiz's homecoming, 1954 (released from Sahiwal Jail)

The jail cell courtyard in Sahiwal Jail, 2017

You were not around much when I was growing up. It was either the prison or the very late nights at the newspaper where you were Chief Editor. I left for school when you were sleeping and I was sleeping when you got home after sending the paper to press.

My childhood was a lonely one. You were not around for almost five years. Mama was constantly under stress from fighting your case in court, to working, to putting food on the table, to handling two growing daughters, one of whom was constantly getting into mischief and asking questions. I don't need to tell you which one that was! I had friends at school but there was always a vacuum, an emptiness in my life which has remained with me. Even today, as I face the twilight of my life, I so wish to ask you to explain to me this crazy world we are living in and how to deal with it without going mad ourselves. I want your warmth, I want your twinkling eyes just to comfort me when the going gets rough. I want your perfume which always swirled around you when you came into the room or when I hugged you.

I don't remember all of my school days, except that they were rough. I wonder if everyone feels the same about their school years. I was a good student but semi-maladjusted, I was fluent in English; not athletic at all; sort of a tom-boy who played tricks on others; made funny remarks about the teachers all the time; was never caught but certainly reprimanded often; liked playing in the servants' quarters when I got home because I had no other playmates and had so much energy to burn.
The days when we travelled to see you in prison were an adventure for me. I remember the long, hot train rides in third class compartments with food in tiffin carriers, sitting with other women packed tightly like sardines as the train jogged along. Mama, because of her fair skin and blue eyes would be stared at throughout the journey. "Where are you going?" was the favourite question asked. "To see my husband," she would say and bottle up. "And where is he?" "In jail", I would pipe up and inevitably get a glare from her.

When you were shifted to Hyderabad jail, it was such an unending journey. It lasted more than 24 hours with many stops on the way. I must now give my mother much credit for holding her end together in such extreme circumstances.

There were times, I recall, when we arrived for the meeting and were told that permission had not been conveyed. She would rant and rave to no avail, and we would have to make the journey back, disappointed and frustrated. I would ask endless questions about why we had not met you and Mama would lose her patience and tell me to be quiet. I would retire to a corner of the compartment, hurt and angry. But then, when I think of it now, she too must have carried that disappointment which probably cut deep into her heart like a knife. My badgering must have made that wound hurt more.
And when we did manage to meet you, it was always such a relief. We would wait in the visitors' room, anxiously, Mama having the packages examined and re-examined by the person in charge. Books, food, cigarettes, clothes, toiletries. Lists were made, signatures taken, and then doors would start clanging. Footsteps would be heard. Sounds of salutes being made and loud voices yelling commands somewhere would reach us. Anticipation would grow with every moment: Cheemie sitting silently waiting and I squirming in my chair. And then the door would open and you would walk in. Calm, smiling, eyes twinkling, sweet smelling, neatly dressed. I would leap up and hug you. Mama and Cheemie would do the same and the clock would start ticking.

I was usually taken out to your cell to keep me occupied. I liked the garden outside your cell. It had roses, planted by you I am told. Your "mushaqati", or sort of valet, was used to seeing me running in, prancing around, chasing a cat or a bird or even a chicken sometimes. He would give me a glass of some sweet drink and I would spend that time just running around playing by myself. Then it would be time to leave. A hug or two and we were back on the train. Mama usually looking out of the train window as the sun went down, and I drooping on her shoulder trying to keep my eyes open.

Do you remember the time I gave your jailer a scolding, which I hope he did not forget for a long time. As we entered the meeting room he said, "We have cooked koftas for you today as you asked". "How do you know I wanted koftas?" I asked. "I read your letter in which you had told your father," he said. I gave him a glare. "You read my letter? You actually read my letter? How could you?" I think he looked sheepish. That is a story which has stuck in my mind for almost sixty five years!

Entering the cell courtyard of Sahiwal Jail after 70 odd years

With the superintendent of Sahiwal Jail, 2017

Then there was the time when I asked you to get me a doll for my birthday. How exactly you were going to make that happen is a good question now, but as an 8-year-old I had the right to make a request to my Abu. I never did get a doll but instead you wrote me a poem. And that poem is among my most precious memories of you. After all, how many daughters can claim they got a poem from their father on their birthday, and that too a father who would one day become a Lenin Peace Prize winner and a Nobel Prize nominee? I am not boasting here (well I could be a bit!), but the fact is a doll would have been chewed up by termite or cockroaches or ants or whatever, but a poem is for posterity.

No, I don't and never have written poetry but I am the daughter of a poet who is still a great favourite and revered by so many.

On so many occasions throughout my life I have faced situations when your name linked to mine has given me respect, love, admiration, even adoration. I have never ever felt worthy of it, of course, but know that at that moment I am just riding the wave but cannot or do not want to get off. I never ever want any person to feel that I have not given them the opportunity to express their love for you to me. I owe you that and I owe them that. At that moment I am your "presence" before them, and I cannot show any emotion except gratitude and humility.

I have shaken hands with Presidents, Royalty, Prime Ministers and icons all over the world but I know it has been you, not me they have saluted, you they have recognized, you they have spoken to.

I am just a representative of the great man called Faiz.
No, I do not write poetry…
There can only be one great poet in the family, and that was you.

Poem

اِک منیزہ ہماری بیٹی ہے

جو بہت ہی پیاری بیٹی ہے

ہم ہی کب اُس کو پیار کرتے ہیں

سب کے سب اُس کو پیار کرتے ہیں

کیسے سب کو نہ آئے پیار اُس پر

ہے وہی تو ہماری ڈکٹیٹر

پیار سے جو بھی جی چُرائے گا

وہ خوب اُس سے مار کھائے گا

خیر یہ بات تو ہنسی کی ہے

ویسے سچ مُچ وہ بہت اچھی ہے

پھول کی طرح اُس کی رنگت ہے

چاند کی طرح اُس کی صورت ہے

جب وہ خوش ہو کر مُسکراتی ہے

چاندنی جگ میں پھیل جاتی ہے

پڑھنے لکھنے میں خوب قابل ہے

کھیلنے کودنے میں کامِل ہے

عمر دیکھو تو آٹھ سال کی ہے

عقل دیکھو تو ساٹھ سال کی ہے

پھر وہ گانا بھی اچھا گاتی ہے

گرچہ تم کو نہیں سُناتی ہے

بات کرتی ہے اِس قدر میٹھی

جیسے ڈالی پہ کُوک بُلبل کی

ہاں کوئی اُس کو جب ستاتا ہے

تب ذرا غصّہ آ ہی جاتا ہے

پر وہ جلدی سے مان جاتی ہے

کب کسی کو بھلا ستاتی ہے

ہے شگُفتہ بہت مزاج اُس کا

سارا عُمدہ ہے کام کاج اُس کا

ہے منیزہ کی آج سالگرہ

ہر طرف شور ہے مبارک کا

چاند تارے دعائیں دیتے ہیں

پھول اُس کی بلائیں لیتے ہیں

باغ میں گا رہی ہے بُلبل

تم سلامت رہو منیزہ گُل

امّاں، ابا اور باجی بھی

آنٹیاں اور بہن بھائی بھی

آج سب اُس کو پیار کرتے ہیں

مِل کے بار بار کہتے ہیں

سو تو ہزار بار آئے

یوں کہو بے شمار بار آئے

لائے ہر بار اپنے ساتھ خوشی

اور ہم سب کہا کریں یونہی

یہ منیزہ ہماری بیٹی ہے

یہ بہت ہی پیاری بیٹی ہے۔

فیض احمد فیض

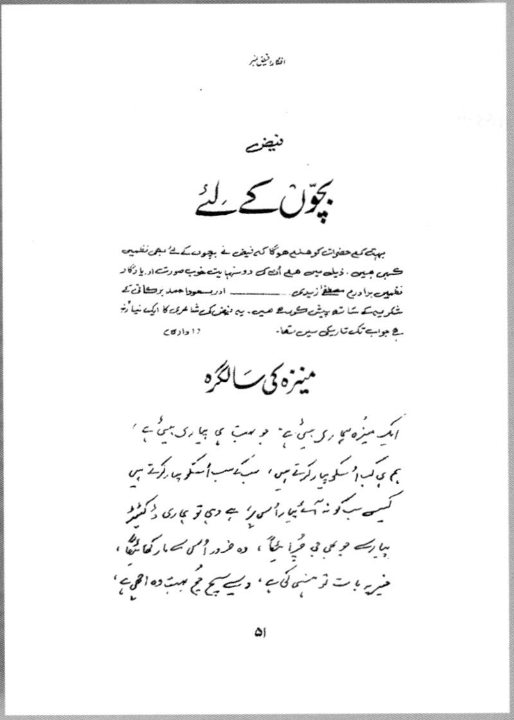

فیض

بچوں کے لئے

بہت کم حضرات کو علم ہوگا کہ فیض نے بچوں کے لئے بھی نظمیں کہی ہیں۔ ذیل میں ہم اُن کی دو نہایت خوبصورت اور یادگار نظمیں برادرم مصطفیٰ زیدی ــــــــ اور مسعود احمد برکاتی کے شکریے کے ساتھ پیش کر رہے ہیں۔ یہ فیض کی شاعری کا ایک نیا رُخ ہے جو اب تک تاریکی میں تھا۔ (ادارہ)

میزہ کی سالگرہ

ایک میزہ ہماری بیٹی ہے، جو بہت ہی پیاری بیٹی ہے،
ہم ہی کب اُسکو پیار کرتے ہیں، سب کے سب اُسکو پیار کرتے ہیں
کیسے سب کو نہ آئے پیار اُس پر ہے وہی تو ہماری ڈکٹیٹر
پیار سے جو بھی جی چُرائیگا، وہ ضرور اُس سے مار کھائیگا،
خیر یہ بات تو ہنسی کی ہے، ویسے سچ مچ بہت وہ اچھی ہے،

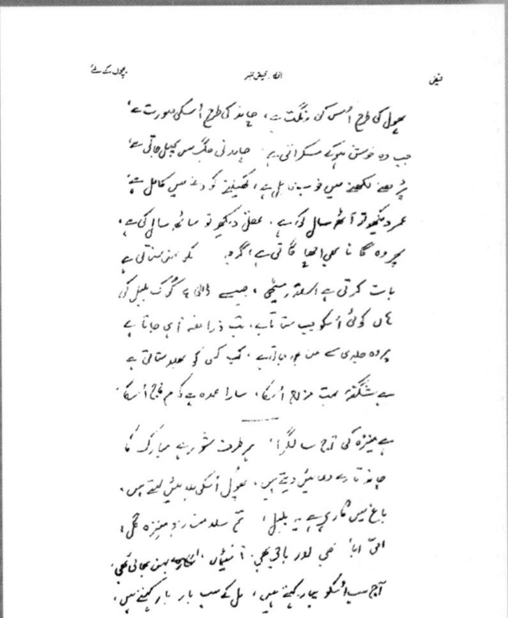

پھول کی طرح اُس کی رنگت ہے، چاند کی طرح اُسکی صورت ہے،
جب وہ خوش ہو کے مسکراتی ہے، چاندنی جگ میں پھیل جاتی ہے،
پڑھنے لکھنے میں خوب چالاک ہے، کھیلنے کودنے میں کامل ہے،
عمر دیکھو تو آٹھ سال کی ہے، عقل دیکھو تو ساٹھ سال کی ہے،
پھر وہ گانا بھی اچھا گاتی ہے، اگر وہ [illegible] کر ہنستی ہے
بات کرتی ہے اسقدر میٹھی، جیسے ڈالی پہ کوک بلبل کی،
ہاں کوئی اُسکو جب ستاتا ہے، تب ذرا غصہ آ ہی جاتا ہے،
پر وہ جلدی سے من بھی جاتی ہے، کب کسی کو بھلا ستاتی ہے،
ہے شگفتہ بہت مزاج اُسکا، سارا عمدہ ہے کام کاج اُسکا،

ہے میزہ کی آج سالگرہ، ہر طرف شور ہے مبارک کا،
چاند تارے دعائیں دیتے ہیں، پھول اُسکی بلائیں لیتے ہیں،
باغ میں گا رہی ہے یہ بلبل، تم سلامت رہو میزہ گُل،
امی ابا بھی اور باجی بھی، آنٹیاں، انکلز، بہن بھائی بھی،
آج سب اُسکو پیار کرتے ہیں، مل کے سب بار بار کہتے ہیں،

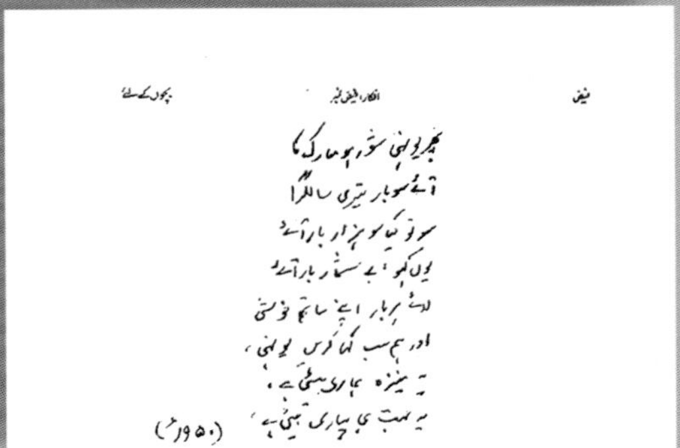

پھر یونہی شور ہو مبارک کا
آئے سو بار تیری سالگرہ
سو تو کیا سو ہزار بار آئے
یوں کہو بے شمار بار آئے
لائے ہر بار اپنے ساتھ خوشی
اور ہم سب کہا کریں یونہی،
یہ میزہ ہماری بیٹی ہے،
یہ بہت ہی پیاری بیٹی ہے،
(۱۹۵۰ء)

Some moments I want to share with you

There is almost a life time I want to share with you and hope you have the patience to hear me out.

Do you remember the times when you would come to Lahore from Karachi and I was in the hostel at Kinnaird College? That must have been the years between September 1962 and summer of 1967 when I appeared for my BA examination.
You would sometimes take me out for lunch with Miss Robinson's permission. She was our hostel warden and a lovely, gentle person. A great psychology teacher too. Well, perhaps I say great because I always topped in her class.

Anyway, in those "stolen" moments, when I actually had you all to myself, we would usually eat a Chinese meal which was such a luxury back then. There was this one place which was operating next to Ferozesons on the Mall, appropriately called Far East. We would order the usual menu of chicken corn soup, egg fried rice and probably beef and chilli or sweet-and-sour prawns. I used to look forward to spending that time alone with you and the food, which was such a pleasant change from the bland hostel food we had to stomach day after day.

And there you would sit smoking away with that dreamy look in your shining eyes. Looking into space, but also at my face, in case I asked you a question or wanted a comment. I would chatter away non-stop about nothing in particular, but about everything that would be bothering me at that time. It could have been a subject, an exam, a person or a teacher, or the heat or the cold or lack of money or Mama's lack of attention, etc. But those are cherished memories of years when I was sort of finding 'myself', exploring the world without any parental stress, learning the rules of life unfettered with a sense of freedom and groping around for affection and friendship all at the same time. I made wonderful friends back then, some of whom are still my closest confidantes. I gained an inner strength which has kept me afloat in the face of so many 'paper tigers'. I experienced an amazing sense of freedom, which I fiercely protect and value to this day. I saw people change colours like autumn leaves. This also taught me valuable lessons of how fickle human nature is, and how stupid it is to trust people at face value. I also learnt that being vulnerable is a weakness; being too trusting a weakness; being too giving a weakness; being too confident a weakness. Actually, being 'too' of anything is not good.

So, I learnt that moderation in every way is the best course, but that realization came much later in life and I learnt lessons the hard way. But then who said life was going to be easy?
You should know.

Anyway, I was telling you about some moments which have remained with me well after they passed and memories of some people who still warm my heart or make it cold with anger. Depending!
I just want to warn you that there is going to be no chronological path that these thoughts will follow.

Like how did I meet Benazir Bhutto? She was a sitting Prime Minister living in that shining white house on top of a hill in Islamabad. Many meetings and moments have just happened in my life and I have sat back to think, "Did that really happen? Was I actually there?"

Interviewing Prime Minister Benazir Bhutto for PTV during her second tenure

Meeting BB was one such magical moment.
I was interviewing many high-profile people for Pakistan Television, women mostly. I included men later. Someone suggested that I meet BB. And I thought," Oh yeah? How exactly does one do that?" But then the permissions came through, the interview was booked, the questions faxed to her office, the outfit to wear selected. It was a crisp autumn morning. The crew was in place on time. Tech tests had been completed. I was wired up. And then rustling sounds started floating through and she literally breezed in. Charming, with a beautiful skin, clever sparkling eyes, alert, smiling. I was introduced by Farhatullah Babar and she immediately recognized your magic name. A connection was made and we talked for over forty minutes. She was pleasant to engage with and was a spontaneous talker. I deviated from my questions but she had no problem with that. We had a cup of tea later and she breezed out. I had had my moment of "glory", a first for PTV, a first for me, a memory that remains clear and fresh even after a lapse of more than thirty years.

The Queen's invitation to attend the annual garden party at Buckingham Palace completely floored me. It came in my capacity as being the only Pakistani woman to have headed the Commonwealth Broadcasting Association for three tenures. I heard the news and thought again, "Who me? Buckingham Palace, where I had been a couple of times after buying a ticket and following groups of tourists? Now I get to go and have tea there? With the Queen of England no less?"

EIIR

The Lord Chamberlain is commanded by Her Majesty to invite

Mrs. Saffina Kossar Ellahi and Mrs. Moneeza Hashmi

to a Garden Party at Buckingham Palace on Thursday, 31st May, 2018 from 4 to 6 p.m.

This card does not admit

Waiting to enter Buckingham Palace as an invited guest to the Queen's birthday celebrations, 2018

But the funniest part is when I shared this news with Zainab, my eldest granddaughter. She heard it as she usually does with a kind of disinterest. When I asked her, "Zainab, do you think I should go? I have to pay my fare and all the expenses as well." That's when she looked up and said with a pretty straight face, "Are you even thinking of not going Dadi? This is Buckingham Palace. This is the Queen of bloody England who is inviting you! What's wrong with you?" I guess I got my answer then and sheepishly looked away. It was one of the most glorious afternoons on Thursday, 31st May 2018 as I waited outside the gates of the Palace for entry. Having checked the weather a hundred times every day for the past week, I was frozen with fear that it might rain, but it did not. It was sunny. It was warm. And the Palace staff was welcoming and smiling. My friend Saffina (you had to have a local host) and I walked through, pinching ourselves literally as we came upon the large grounds decorated with buntings, a band playing live music; throngs of people, dressed in their 'Sunday best' just like us, milling around; drinks being served by liveried waiters. The sun played hide and seek with the clouds all afternoon. The bushes and flowers were meticulously manicured and their perfume followed us as we walked around. There were carefree but excited vibes all over as people waited for Her Majesty's appearance. The band struck up "God Save the Queen" and everyone stood still as she came out and stood attentive on the porch in turquoise blue. Prince William followed close behind. She walked among the people greeting some as she walked to her pavilion, an example of decorum and dignity. It was such a show of British traditions and heritage. She walked by. I caught a glimpse of her face which did not show any emotion, facing at least 1,500 strangers all pressing forward. At ninety four years, she was as steady as they come, on her feet. The tea served was sumptuous. Of course paper thin cucumber sandwiches and the famous English scones. On the drive home, in a moment of reflection, I thought, "Lady you did well. The Queen of England and a personalized invitation to her garden party. Not many in Pakistan can boast of that." But then, how many receive the Lenin Prize and that also includes you, my dear father!

Faiz receiving the Lenin Peace Prize, Moscow 1962

It was 1995 and I had gotten a fellowship to go to the US: sixteen states in three weeks and all expenses paid. It was a fantastic trip in which we got to travel across the country. But perhaps what I can recall as the defining moment is sitting down to dinner with George Bush Senior (former President of the USA). Before that, all the delegates from several countries had a round table with him and I was selected to pose a one-on-one question to him. And mine was, can you guess?

"Why is there no female President of USA when Pakistan has a female PM Benazir Bhutto, as do Sri Lanka, Bangladesh and Israel (at the time)?" He gave a wishy-washy answer. "Well we don't discourage it. We are an equal playing field. Women should come forward," At dinner he said to me, "Lady, you asked a tough question and caught me off guard," and then laughed it off. We all did. Later that evening, I had my hand shaken by several of the female guests present. I guess it was a good question. Several years later we know the result of what happened when a female did try to stand as USA president. She won the election but lost the White House. Doesn't make sense. That's politics.

A few years later I received an email that bowled me over. Yet again. It takes quite a lot for that to happen. When I read that I was being given a special award by NHK in Tokyo in the presence of His Royal Highness the Crown Prince of Japan (who is now King by the way), you could have knocked me down with a feather, literally. I had been out of 'active' service of TV for many years and was sort of 'retired' from that sphere. I was quietly carrying on my grandmotherly duties with an odd consultancy here and there. And then comes this super prestigious award from NHK which is the giant of broadcasting in Asia. So, with all expenses paid, I landed in Tokyo in the autumn of 2015. On D-Day we were given the schedule of the award ceremony and the entire procedure. We were three awardees, myself, Dr Milton Chen from USA, who is one of the pioneers of Sesame Street and Mr George Auckland Former Head of Innovation, BBC Learning (UK).

The meeting with the royal guest was before the ceremony so we were taken to a side room and given strict instructions on how to address the guest. We were not to initiate any conversation with him. We were not to shake hands unless he put out his hand. We were not to drag any discussion with him beyond 30 seconds. We were to remain silent as he spoke to the other people in the circle. And we were not to ask for any photographs to be taken.

We stood silent and slightly nervous as he moved slowly around the large circle. The conversation going on between him and each guest was barely beyond a whisper. The Japanese, as we know, are extremely particular about following instructions to the letter and get very agitated if any rule is broken or tampered with. So when he walked up to me and I was introduced as a Pakistani delegate, he sort of looked mildly interested. Malala had won the Nobel Prize just two days before. I just elaborated, "I am from the country of Malala, your Royal Highness". Now that got his attention and he started speaking about girls' education and how important it was for girls to be given a place in all spheres of life and in the government. I kept nodding away until I saw his aide behind him looking horrified at the amount of time this conversation was taking. It was throwing off the entire schedule. But Japanese being Japanese, and that too in the presence of Royalty, I felt really sorry for the guy who was probably thinking as to how he was going to make up the extra three minutes this conversation was taking.

With awardees of NHK President's award, Tokyo, Japan 2015

That part being over and after I had had my moment with the Royalty of Japan, we were herded back into the studio for the award ceremony, where the Crown Prince watched along with the invited audience. My speech was 40 seconds long instead of 30 seconds so that is also something I must live with, a rule breaker of NHK. Maybe that explains why I have not been invited back since then.

There have been several PMs and Presidents of Pakistan who I have met, talked to, shook hands with. A life in PTV gives you these opportunities. When I was presented with my Pride of Performance Award in 2002, that is the closest I ever got to a military man handing it to me. I knew Gen. Musharraf personally (as you might know) when he was a young man studying in FC College. He is a cousin of one of my dearest friends, so I met him off and on at family events. He was rising slowly in the Pakistan Army, but that was of no consequence to me. Until that one morning when, after I had directed and executed the Kargil show on PTV Lahore as General Manager, I got a phone call from him, or rather from his office. I remember it was in the morning and I was in Sant Nagar, where I would go off and on to supervise a public school activities.

Chief of Army staff wants to talk to me? Seriously? And then he was on the line.
"Thank you Moneeza," he said, "for the marvellous show PTV put on last night for the 'Heroes of Kargil', who now stand vindicated," he said. I did my usual thank you Sir, very kind of you bit. And then sat down, a bit shaken.

He also sent me a short note of thanks, written on his official card, which of course I have misplaced. I am totally hopeless at keeping or saving interesting or historic documents. I have no result sheets of the boys or mine anywhere. Important photos from the past are lost. No degrees anywhere. I even once threw away Ali's matric result in the garbage, and it was saved because the sweepers that day were late! It is still a standing joke in the family.

Anyway, so the card is nowhere to be found and I am rather glad it's lost, because after reading Naseem Zehra's book From Kargil to the Coup, I am not sure that the show was something I would be proud of. Sure, we paid homage to the jawans and brave men who died in Kargil, but for what reason were they sent to their deaths and what was that conflict about? She exposes the entire story of a mismanaged confrontation with India, and the then Prime Minister of Pakistan (an elected one I may add) having no idea about it or having given permission for it. What a tragedy, and what a huge waste of lives and loss of national integrity, when Nawaz Sharif went scurrying to DC to ask Bill Clinton to save Pakistan's face and reputation. Sad is not the word for it.
I believe I am the only person (to date) in this family, after yourself, to have seen all the following three greats face-to-face.

Receiving President of Pakistan's
Pride of Performance Award, 2003

I have 'met' Ho Chi Minh in Hanoi. I have 'met' Lenin in Moscow. I have 'met' Mao in Beijing.
And what amazing experiences they all were, just walking past them as quickly as my feet would allow me, because the guards around, with their dead pan, totally inhuman expressions and stiff no nonsense looks and no eye contact seemed to want us to get on and get out.

But the awe I felt at being in the presence of these giants was an unmatched experience.
They had changed the history of the world of their times.

These men were the actual super heroes, not Batman or Captain Marvel flying around.
I had read somewhere that when you were asked about your religion, you replied, "Mine is the same as Rumi's."

Somehow that remark stuck in my mind for years.
When a group of friends and ex-students started planning a trip to Turkey, "I will come only if you take me to Konya," was my answer.

And so there I stood, after an eight-hour gruelling bus ride on that glorious August morning in Konya, before the Mevlana, wondering what was it that made him and the likes of him live on through people like you.

That visit to Konya is a highlight I would like to repeat. I want to breathe that air again. I want to swirl (as much as I can now!) again. I want to feel that presence again. Ah, Mevlana! Yes, you are, all about love, peace, giving, sharing and inclusivity.
When I found out that Adeel and Samer were having a baby girl (I had to get secret information out of the gynaecologist without their knowing), and that they had selected Zainab to be her name, I was overcome with emotion and a passion to visit Hazrat Bibi Zainab's tomb in Damascus and thank her for this gift. The more I read about Bibi Zainab, the more moved I was by her fight against the murderers of her family. She was the first feminist of Islam, and the world, for me. The strength of her courage, the power of her diction in Yazeed's court, the command over herself during those terrible times of pulling her family out of chaos, is what inspires me. The leadership qualities she displayed, on her march to Syria after the tragedy, made me want to present myself to her in person in Damascus, and bow my head in reverence as a token of my admiration and love. I felt a connection with this wonderful woman.

I get an odd feeling whenever I am in such places which I hold sacred and dear in my heart and mind and then suddenly they are in front of me. I felt it inside the Dome in Al Aqsa. I felt it in Ajmer Sharif the first time I visited there. I felt it every time I entered the great mosque in Madina. I felt it in the Cathedral in Seville. I felt it in front of the statue of the Pieta in Rome. I felt it as I walked around your cell in Sahiwal, almost six decades after you had left it. I felt it in Pakpattan Shareef. I felt it praying at Sachal Sarmast's grave. It's odd, isn't it? I can give you many more examples of this surreal feeling that washes over me and then leaves me with a strange sense of peace.
I must tell you about my trip to Kabul which was purely by coincidence and by chance, but in another letter.

I want to tell you about another event I was invited to, which has stayed with me all these years.

"Why are you going to Chhattisgarh?" asked Pappu Mahesh when I told her I was coming. "It's not safe," she said. That got me thinking, and what do I discover? It is bang in the middle of Naxalite area with Marxist conflicts on a regular basis. Dr Arfa Syeda, a dear friend, was my companion for this visit. Off we went across Wagah and caught the plane to Chhattisgarh.

Receiving Faiz Centenary Souvenir from the President of India, Delhi 2011

We found out that the head of police there was the grandson of the poet Firaq Ghorakhpuri and wanted to hold this event as a token of his appreciation to the two of you. I remember a feeling of unease throughout our drive to the rest house. I remember military militia at every intersection; the patrolling of armed guards in the rest house, and the many guards who stood outside our door, vigilant. It was eerie.

The next morning, in the huge hall which was full of invited guests, the arrival of the chief of police as chief guest was heralded by armed guards, who came and manned every window and door of that auditorium. The chief guest walked in, breezily dressed in a simple coat and trouser, quite at ease, greeting some of the VIPs and joined us on stage. I was tense throughout that morning. All for the love of you and peace between India and Pakistan, I could not get on the plane the next morning fast enough, trying not to look at the guards who drove me to the airport and escorted me to the plane itself.

I do get into odd places as you can see because I have friends in high places!
By the way, how many Nobel Prize winners have you met?
I've met three.

Let's start with the first.
It usually begins with a phone call, doesn't it?
I remember that phone call you received, in 1962. Yes, you were reclining on a sofa-cum-bed at 41 Empress Road. The phone instrument was one of those black ones in which you had to turn the dial every time you dialled a number. Remember them? So, the phone rang. It was late in the afternoon. I was just hanging out looking down from the terrace into the garden downstairs where we were never allowed to play, but then that's another story. You answered it and your facial expression changed as you spoke. I turned around and saw Mama standing over you. "What is it Faiz?" she asked. You were recovering from a heart attack and recuperating those days, so I guess she was rightly worried because the expression on your face was odd to say the least. You did not answer immediately and she asked again, "Is it the Nobel Prize?" Why did she ask that particular question has evaded me all these years. Was there a conversation happening in which you had been or were being nominated? Anyway, you looked at her, quite lost for a moment, and I recall your words to this day. Remember we are talking 1962! You said, "No. Bigger than that!" I cannot remember my immediate reaction to those words. But then that black phone started ringing and ringing and

ringing. And a short while later people started coming and thronging around you. That is when I was told to go to my room by Mama.
The rest is history. 1962 Lenin Peace Prize.

I looked up to see who the others were who had been given this award. The names are overwhelming. Among many others, I see Fidel Castro, Pablo Picasso, Indira Gandhi, Mahmoud Darvesh, Aruna Asif Ali, Angela Davis (I remember meeting her in Moscow in 1985 at the World Conference for Women).

Anyway, I digress as usual but what I was saying was about a phone call. That's how many of my life's defining moments have begun or ended.

So, I get this phone call that Mother Teresa is in town and can I do an interview with her. Surprisingly, she was visiting one of her homes in Model Town, around the corner from our house. It was the time of Zia ul Haq so I guess they wanted it quiet and subdued. I rang up Nyla Daud, my close friend, a journalist, to accompany me and off we went. I stood before this pint-sized, wizened old lady (who was later declared a saint) and asked her a few silly questions, the usual type of what message she would like to give to people in general, etc. She spoke gently and softly, gave me a pendant with an impression of Christ, and also a card on which she wrote a message for me. I have lost both these prized possessions, but I do remember the message on the card was about the power of prayer. That message I have held onto all my life.

Dr Abdus Salam's visit also miraculously happened and we had a jam-packed Pearl Continental Hotel hall that morning. I cannot for the life of me remember how I managed to swing that one! Seriously, a Nobel Prize scientist comes to deliver a Faiz Memorial lecture, on what topic you may ask? One day I got this idea that I had to invite him. How I did do that escapes me. No WhatsApp. No cell phones. I recall a letter I wrote to him in Trieste which obviously reached him and he agreed to come. From there on, the whole visit just rolled on via remote management. What I do recall clearly is that when his rather biggish vehicle entered the hotel, there were security guards who were running along it as it slowed down. I was waiting at the front entrance to receive him. He greeted me most graciously and we went into the hall where the applause was deafening! Again, guards took up posts next to the doors, which for me was quite disconcerting, as the whole Ahmadi scenario had not quite sunk in, nor the threats he may be facing in a public forum. Anyway, the talk went smoothly. He was applauded again as he left and I am totally indebted to this great man, who, on a whimsical invitation from me came to Lahore and honoured your memory. Even now when I read his talk it goes over my head, frankly, but then a lot of sensible stuff does. I guess I am just not wired that way. Totally practical and managerial, yes. But intellectual and academic? A big no!

Greeting Mother Teresa, Lahore 1991

Meeting Nobel Prize winner
Malala Yousafzai, Birmingham 2017

And then there is Malala.
I met her when she was a young 16 year old. A timid sort of person. I landed up at her house in Birmingham with my dear friend Sally Ann. She and her family came out to greet us. It had been a long straight drive from Glasgow. I was exhausted and hungry too. The meeting had been set up by mutual friends. Her dad and I had the usual conversation about you and how much he valued your thoughts, etc. He spoke about his connection to your values. It was a pleasant evening. Malala throughout sat quietly in a corner sofa, just looking on. I gave her a copy of my book and we had a photo op, and then I took the train to London. The next time I met her was in the summer of 2017 when I took my granddaughters Alina and Zainab to meet her in Birmingham. This time she had won the Nobel Prize and there was a marked difference in her demeanour. She was more confident and chirpier. She spoke to the girls about her winning the prize and what it meant to her. The girls were tickled pink to be in her company and she gave them autographed copies of her book which they cherish to this day and have read many times over!

So that makes my count of three Nobel Laureates under my belt!
Meeting the President of India again was not such a big affair. We were invited to attend your centennial celebrations in New Delhi and she hosted the Pakistan
delegation. We were given awards and certificates. She spoke to each of us graciously and thanked us for coming. Adeel was also with me on that trip.

At a dinner with Dr Abdul Salam, Lahore 1985

Taking Zainab and Alina to meet Malala Yousafzai, Birmingham 2017

Meeting Presidents and Prime Ministers of Pakistan became a routine affair in PTV. As General Manager I would be there to organize the event. The minute your name was mentioned, the VIPs would stand to attention or say a word or two of how much they appreciated your poems, etc., and suddenly my presence would take on a surreal vibe, and the lackeys would also stand to attention!

And then there was Dilip Kumar, who came to pay his condolences when he was invited to Pakistan on a state visit. I had met him previously in Mumbai, several years earlier, fulfilling my life-long dream of actually laying eyes on this chocolate hero of my youth! And then to see him in our very own living room, sitting on the floor as we talked. Saira Banu sat on the sofa with Ali, while he and I talked about--- what? My memory fails me again!

I could go on and on about the wonderful people who changed my life in one meeting or who made me feel special to be in their company for those precious moments. And always the connection of course led to you.

Be it Benazir Bhutto or Dr Abdus Salaam or Roshan Ara Begum or Madam Noor Jahan or Dilip Kumar or Abida Parveen or President Prathiba Patil or President Mamnoon Hussain or Bilquis Edhi or Hanan Ashrawi or Naseeruddin Shah or Shabana Azmi or ... and the list is endless. All roads lead to you and the love and respect for you. For that, I bow my head in gratitude.

Talking to Dilip Kumar during his visit to condole the death of Faiz, Lahore, 1984

Spending a lifetime in PTV

I wonder if you remember that afternoon when you and I were sitting in the audience at the PTV Karachi station launch ceremony. You had been invited by Zufiqar Ali Bokhari, who was appointed as the first General Manager of PTV Karachi, and I just tagged along because I had told you a couple of times I wanted to join PTV. Having recently given my BA examinations I was at a loose end. It being summer holidays I was in Karachi where I had no friends anyway. We were sitting in the front seats, since I guess you were always given a priority seat when you entered any arena. I recall next to us was Altaf Gauhar, a good friend of yours, and who was Secretary, Information at the time. He got up to greet someone and I tugged at your sleeve and whispered, "Abba. Ask him". When he sat down again you said to him, "Bhai. Yeh hamari beti TV join karna chahti hai" (Our daughter wants to join PTV), and looked away as if you had nothing to do with either my asking or his reply. I can't remember his answer but he did glance at me kindly and asked a couple of peripheral questions. The programme started and all conversation ceased. I am sure you must have been relieved too.

A few days later I received a telegram (yes, those were the days of telegrams and booked trunk calls), instructing me to report to the Chaklala School for TV training in Rawalpindi after two weeks, and my long association with PTV began.

The barracks of Chaklala, where our training was held, were pretty dilapidated in those days. We had German instructors. The equipment now appears terribly outdated. Even back then too it was not too impressive. The studio was small and quite dingy. The hours were long and arduous but the work was fascinating and exciting. I made life-long friends. The ones still alive I am in touch with, and the ones who passed away, I recall with fond memories and a tug at my heart. There was laughter. There was leg pulling.

Khawateen Time Awards, PTV Lahore

There were rivalries and competition. But it was all camaraderie. Fun. Bonding. We were pioneers in a new field. We were going to be the first to make that magic screen come alive. We were going to educate, inform and entertain. We held that power on our finger tips to make fantasy become a reality. And the other way around.
Yes, those were exciting days of adventure, flirtation, independence.

October 1967 saw me in Lahore and I joined PTV Lahore as Assistant Producer.
You were with me for most of my journey after that. There were good days and bad days, frustrating as well as exhilarating ones. Days when I was praised for my hard work, and days when I was chastised simply because I spoke up to the wrong person at the wrong time in public. You know me, right? I was never one to mince my words. I am learning now to do so in my seventieth decade! You will be surprised how cooll and dumb I can appear in public, sitting through hours of absolute rubbish happening on stage and practicing what you told me years ago. I switch off. I suppose some of it has to do with my brain cells becoming slower and quieter, but some of it is due to instinctively following your advice.

The years in PTV went on. Sometimes painful, sometimes fun, some ups, some downs. But it has been a career in which I carved a name for myself, a reputation of being a professional, a straight transparent officer and a responsible worker. There were no nights or hours in PTV. There were no holidays or off days when an assignment was due. There were no short-cuts or slip-ups. The screen was your test. It could make or break you. There were times when I was criticized heavily for my work. There were objections raised in the Parliament about my presentations. There were explanations demanded from me regarding my non-conformist behaviour, my lack of protocol, my absence of paying homage to authority who in my opinion did not deserve it anyway. My total disregard of discipline when it came to attending nonsensical meetings, and listening to the pathetic rants of an inept high command, listening to endless rhetoric from mouthpieces of government sycophants. I would either not go or switch off, look bored, totally disinterested or make snide remarks, sometimes loud enough to be heard all around. I was never reprimanded, but my promotions were held up, trips for training abroad passed me over, my duties were punishments,, my work hours were increased.

Yes, I paid some heavy dues for not suppressing my inner self of justice. I suffered many a time for not performing according to rules. I was harassed. But you know me and my personality and the values I hold dear.
I am no quitter. That's why you saw a 'dictator' in me when I was eight years old. You saw a soldier fighting on for her rights. You knew me well even though we continued to be separated most of our lives.
PTV moulded me in many ways, both negatively and positively. I learnt to handle being in the limelight. I learnt to face blatant misogyny and gender discrimination. I learnt to never let praise go to my head, but take it as a step forward towards achieving better. By the same yardstick, I never let victimization cloud my vision. I saw through the hate and evil in some faces, and I fought them head on. I confronted them, challenged them, called them out in a discreet manner, tore down their façade of self-righteousness, and exposed them openly.

Yes. Those were moments when I missed you the most. Your calmness, your aura, your voice, your warmth, your presence.

But I learnt to survive it all single-handedly, and probably that is what moulded me into the person I now am.

I take leaps of faith and somehow survive! Do I get that instinct from Mama or you is the question that I am seeking an answer to.

There have been moments in my PTV life which I recall with pride and elation and conversely some with horror and pain. It is a peculiar state to be in.
Let me elaborate a bit more for you.

Just before Mama died in 2003, I had been unceremoniously removed as General Manager, PTV Lahore, because I had been awarded the President's Pride of Performance due to my own 'efforts'. I do not deny I had made a few calls, spoken to some friends, pleaded my case, and a final decision was taken to award me that coveted medal by President Musharraf. Obviously this was not the usual manner in which these decisions were taken. I had not followed protocol, nor begged a few unsavoury people enroute. I believed I deserved it. I believed I had worked for it. I believed I was a suitable candidate and viola! The phone call came congratulating me as I was on my way to the shrine of Data Sahib to pay my respects.

You always used to sort of make fun of me and my "faith". You once said, "Bhai yeh hum sab kay gunah muaaf karway gi." (She will have all our sins forgiven.) Remember? Well. I am a firm believer. And I have faith that when I push hard enough it happens. Is it me? Is it my efforts? Is it that the cosmos is aligned with my cause or is it a Higher Force? Who can say.

Anyway, a few weeks later Mama died, and I get a phone call on my cell phone. This is mid-March, 2003. The caller is President Musharraf, who is calling to condole Mama's demise, since he knows me from bygone years when we were young, and also since Mama was his wife's supervisor/trainer many years earlier in Karachi. I am a bit stunned, and listened to the usual words of consolation and gave the normal answers. And then suddenly the conversation takes a new turn. "Moneeza, I hear you are having some problems in PTV. What happened?" Out comes my story. How I was removed from GM-ship because I was becoming, maybe, too independent. Maybe the Lahore Centre was doing too well. Maybe it was too clean. Maybe the Union was being put in its place and told to mind their business. Maybe I was running it with an iron hand. Maybe I was restricting entry to the station of unsuitable people. Maybe I was just not allowing myself to be pushed, bullied, and stepped on.

Anyway, he heard me out and then said, and here's the surprise for me, "You are due for a promotion I am told?" Sure I am, but who will give it to me, I think. "Yes sir, but that would need me to move to Islamabad". "So what's the problem? We need you here".
And that was it. I took a dive and said, "Yes sir" and a month or so later I was in Islamabad as the first female Director Programmes of PTV. It was a huge jump for me professionally, personally, emotionally, physically and logistically.
I was fortunate to have Samer, Adeel's wife, to take over the running of the house in Lahore.

I placed myself in the thick of a totally male environment.
I had no place to stay and am so thankful to Simi Raheal and her husband (Humair's nephew), for giving me shelter as a guest in their house for eleven months, but the evenings were lonely.

I commuted to Lahore every Friday evening and came back every Monday morning for months on end. Sometimes by car, sometimes by air, if I had the money, sometimes hitching a ride with someone.
Yes it was arduous. But once I had taken up the challenge I was not throwing it away without a fight.

I look at that period as satisfying but extremely draining. I worked long hours, I ate alone, walked alone, watched TV alone, slept alone.

But at the end of each day, I was already planning the next one. Strategizing. Designing. Creating.

And then, like all good things and times, this period also came to an end. Conspiracies brewed and the back stabbing continued. Enmities came to the forefront and jealousies turned into harmful allegations. I was unceremoniously removed, transferred to another department, took early retirement and finally called it a day.

But before that there were so many other incidents I want to recount that you don't know about.
The PTV Union at the time was run by for example bullies, thugs, sell outs, manipulators, you name it. Just monstrous people! Not all of them, but always the ones who wielded the most authority, who had the power to throw their weight around, who yelled the loudest and who terrorized the females and all the 'decent' employees into silence. How I loathed dealing with them because I could see the tactics they used for harassing me. But I was too fearful of taking them on until that one horrible day in August 2003.

The Pride of Performance awards had been announced and I knew it was causing many hearts burn, especially to the ones at the top of the organization who I had bypassed. There was a swearing-in of the PTV's newly elected office bearers, with the Information Minister to administer the oath. As GM I was obviously required to give all the necessary protocol to the Minister and his entourage, but what I could not envisage was the conspiracy afoot to embarrass me in front of him. There have been times in my life when I have been off guard by the situation at hand and taken a fall, later to understand that I was played. But then I guess I do have a naive side to me, which at times prevents me from seeing through people's ill intentions. Anyway, so instead of moving to the studio where the ceremony was to be held, the whole group was herded to the Union office. Again I did not understand or question why we were going there. As we stood around the Union office, the recently elected Union President started telling the Minister of the nepotism I was carrying out by giving Adeel Hashmi, my son, undue preference in PTV appearances. I looked puzzled as Adeel had not appeared in a single PTV programme in my entire tenure except in one talk show as a guest. Then he started a rant, giving a horrible portrayal of me as an officer, how mean I was, how vicious and vindictive, and how totally partisan to some groups and people. I stood listening horrified at this baseless harangue against me. The Minister also listened and then simply said, "I think this warrants an inquiry. I suggest you put all these complaints on a piece of paper with proof and I will look into it." But not before two people, (only two), out of a lot of at least eighty crowded into that room spoke up in my favour and said these were all lies.

I was the best officer they had ever served with and there were some vested interests, in stating these allegations in public. I suddenly saw the light, and knew in an instant that this whole charade was arranged and designed to discredit me in front of the Minister. But I kept my peace. I am deeply indebted to those two colleagues, for having the courage to speak out publicly in my defence. I knew the bullying tactics employed by the Union office bearers and I am sure they took my two supporters to task later. But to date, their words are firmly etched in my brain and I am grateful. It is not easy to stand up and be counted. Having been through those harrowing moments I know the price one pays for speaking one's mind with honesty and transparency. I know the agony of being ostracized and shunned, only because your heart and mind will not accept silence as an option or a way out of a sticky situation.

Later that evening, when I was utterly distraught at what had happened, I received a call from the Minister telling me how he had seen through the whole game of discrediting me. He told me his interpretation of who was behind this façade, and how I should be warned of these evil forces at play.

I cried that evening. I cried hard for all the effort I had put in to put PTV Lahore on the map again. For all the late hours I spent in the office neglecting my home, my friends, and my family only so I could carry out my responsibilities with dedication and honesty. I gave up time for myself, just so that I would be available to the duties assigned. And was this my reward? Public disdain, public blame and blatant lies. But as always, the next day saw me more determined than before. I was in office on time and it was business as usual. I am no quitter and I was not starting now.

You know me. I also had to know the truth of what actually conspired that day. Several years later after my retirement, I met with one of the office bearers of the Union of the time. Over a cup of tea in a congenial atmosphere, he told me how I had been scapegoated and who had been behind it and who paid who to make those allegations against me. It was only then that I finally had closure to that incident. I finally understood the identities of my opponents and their intentions and vested interests. I realized how many enemies I had made simply by being honest, transparent and devoted to integrity as had been inadvertently the role modelled by you. I continued to meet those people socially, looking them in the eye, smiling falsely at their comments but knowing the meanness in their hearts.

There are several incidents which stand out, in those forty odd years of my PTV career. There were great icons I met and rubbed shoulders with, as well as celebrities such as poets, singers, dancers, politicians, sportsmen, foreign and domestic VIPs. Such was the nature of my work.

Some moments etched in my mind are: the Islamic Summit when I saw all the iconic Heads of State coming to Pakistan; Bhutto pronouncing the recognition of Bangladesh; at the Wagah border watching the bus bringing Prime Minister of India, Vajpayee, to Lahore; at the Wagah border watching the POWs from India crossing over into Pakistan; at PTV Station Lahore, when an armoured car raced in after the Pervez Musharraf coup; in the studio when PTV went colour; in the studio when PTV World was launched; at the "inquisition" conducted by a Military General after the takeover of PTV by the Union in 1978; at the PTV awards in Shalimar Gardens during my tenure and so on.

My last meeting with Bano Qudsia, Lahore

These may not be moments of any interest to you but have played a huge part in my journey through the years. I have grown, matured and hopefully become a better professional and human being because of these moments of 'glory' and 'trials'. Some of the wounds still twist and turn my gut. Recalling some of the 'highs' still gives me moments of delirious joy. Some instances still make me cringe in embarrassment. Some make me laugh. Some make me smile. Some bring memories of friends departed. Some bring relief. Some contentment.

But all in all it has been quite a journey of enlightenment, where I learnt so much about people, their pettinesses, their strengths, their unabashed self-projections, their dishonesty, their unbelievable desire for revenge, their harassment of the female gender, their abilities to lie unabashedly, their talent of twisting the facts in their favour, their desire to remain relevant, their sinking to the lowest depths.
And yet I have met people of great stature and dignity and often just one meeting with them has left a lasting impression on my memory. These memories take me to Benazir Bhutto, when I interviewed her for the first time on PTV; to Zulfiqar Ali Bhutto strutting into PTV studios Lahore to declare Ahmadis a minority, (a decision which affected the lives of thousands of people and also took the lives of hundreds of innocent people); to Madam Noor Jahan, sweeping in with her perfume trailing after her, glittering with diamonds, smiling at all who passed her that day accompanied by Achi, her favourite assistant scuttling after her with her make-up and water; to witnessing temper tantrums of so many artistes, singers, performers, anchors over too warm a glass of water or too cold a cup of tea or a late pick up from home or a fused bulb delaying the recording. And so on.

The 'Me Too' movement protesting harassment of women at the hands of the high and the mighty often takes me to so many times when I myself have had to suffer it at the hands of so many who are now old or gone from this world.

I never let you know about the trials I faced in this esteemed organisation until now. I just did not feel like dragging you through it. Was it cowardice or a fear of owning up to what I was feeling and then feeling belittled and degraded at the same time? I never told anyone. It remained bottled up inside of me, but certainly made me stronger for the next onslaught. My armour just became tougher a bit more. My neck stretched a bit more. My back straightened a bit more. The scale on my resolution to fight back went up. Yes. I was ready.

I think in this I am more your daughter than Mama's, although she too remained a fighter all her life. But the-never-give-up, move-ahead-with-focus-and-determination, eyes-front, in-control-most-of-the-time attitude, comes more from you.
You did it with grace and dignity. I do it with a bit more aggression.
You did it weaving a way through. I do it straight between the eyes.
You did it gently. I do it passionately, and passion is always consuming, wild,
exhausting.

But the end result I guess is all that matters.
You remain who you are, respected by even your enemies.
Despite all the trials, I can say that I made significant contributions to the profession, and put in endless efforts to raise its image nationally and globally.

Letter

003 /79
Moscow
14 / 07 / 1979

Dear Mizu,

I received your letter after so many days. It made me happy especially because finally your ordeal is over and now you have the assignment of your taste. Now I hope you will not proceed to entangle yourself in building the house and then get worked up all over again. You cannot change anybody's temperament but still if one tries one can be sensible. And having good sense means that worry never solved a problem. The best thing to do when faced by a problem is to try and solve the issue and simultaneously 'switch off'. Whatever will be, will be. There is no point is fretting and cribbing over it. My own prescription is the one I am using in Beirut, which is that when the sound of falling bombs can be heard overhead, I muffle myself up in the bedclothes, turn a side and go to sleep! My friends have often asked me how I managed to sleep amidst all the noise? I tell them that if one concentrates on the mind, that is, works up one's willpower and makes up the mind to do something, success is bound to be round the corner. Anyway the house will also be constructed, just like this job has been
accomplished. It is better if you start the construction after the rains so that we are also home by then. Your mother has threatened that she will not stay there for as long as the construction thing is going to last. We shall see to that later.

I have been in the hospital for nearly two weeks and the doctors have prodded me inside out. (I have made quite a friend of my lady doctor because she had been looking after me last year also and it is her express instruction that I am to walk up to her even if I so much as sneeze). I will be freed from here next week and then I intend to come to London. I have no idea where we exactly will put up in London. There are quite a few invitations but Iftikhar Arif's is one permanent address and you know him.

C /o Iftikhar Arif
Urdu Markaz, 28 Sackville Street
Piccadilly, London

Prayers for Humair. Love to Ali and Adeel. Ask them what they would like from London.

خط

003 /79
Moscow
14 / 07 / 1979

پیاری میزو

بہت دنوں بعد تمہارا خط ملا، بہت مسرت ہوئی۔ خاص طور سے اس چیز سے کہ آخر تمہاری آزمائش ختم ہوئی اور تمہیں اپنی مرضی کا کام بھی مل گیا۔ اب ایسا نہ ہو کہ اس کے بعد تم گھر بنانے کا درد سر لے کر بیٹھ جاؤ اور پھر چھوٹی موٹی بات پر پریشان ہوتی پھرو۔ کسی کا مزاج تو کوئی نہیں بدل سکتا پھر بھی انسان کوشش کرے تو کچھ تھوڑا بہت تو عقل سے کام لے ہی سکتا ہے۔ اور عقل کی بات یہ ہے کہ محض پریشان ہونے سے تو کوئی مسئلہ حل ہو نہیں سکتا۔ بہتر یہی ہے کہ جب کوئی پریشانی کا مضمون پیدا ہو تو اسے دور کرنے کی کوشش کے ساتھ ساتھ انسان کچھ switch off بھی کرلے کہ جو ہونا ہے سو ہونا ہے رونے دھونے سے کیا فائدہ۔ اپنا نسخہ تو یہ ہے جو ہم بیروت میں بھی استعمال کرتے رہے کہ جب بم گرنے کی آواز زیادہ قریب سے آنے لگتی تو ہم منہ سر لپیٹ کر سو جاتے تھے۔ ہمارے ساتھی اکثر پوچھتے تھے کہ تم اتنے شور میں سو کیسے جاتے ہو۔ ہم نے بتایا کہ انسان اپنے پورے دماغ پر زور ڈال کر یعنی will power کو کام میں لا کر کچھ بھی ٹھان لے تو کسی نہ کسی حد تک کامیاب ہو ہی جاتا ہے۔ خیر جیسے یہ کام ہو گیا گھر بھی بن ہی جائے گا، لیکن اب برسات کے بعد ہی شروع کرو تو اچھا ہے تاکہ ہم بھی گھر پہنچ جائیں۔ کیونکہ تمہاری امی نے دھمکی دی ہے کہ جب تک گھر بننے کا شور شرابہ جاری رہے گا وہ وہاں پر نہیں رہیں گی۔ چلو دیکھا جائے گا۔

ہم قریباً دو ہفتے سے یہاں ہسپتال میں ہیں۔ ڈاکٹر لوگ سب کچھ الٹ پلٹ کر دیکھ چکے ہیں۔ (ہماری ڈاکٹرنی نے تو ہم سے بہت سی دوستی بھی کر رکھی ہے۔ اس لئے کہ پچھلے سال بھی یہی دیکھ بھال کر رہی تھیں اور اس کا اصرار ہے کہ ہمیں چھینک بھی آئے تو سیدھے اس کے پاس چلے آیا کریں۔)

اگلے ہفتے یہاں سے چھٹی ملے گی اور پھر لندن آنے کا ارادہ ہے۔ وہاں کا ٹھکانہ ابھی ٹھیک سے معلوم نہیں۔ دعوت کئی طرف سے ہے لیکن ایک مستقل پتہ افتخار عارف کے دفتر کا ہے جسے تم جانتی ہو۔

C /o Iftikhar Arif
Urdu Markaz, 28 Sackville Street
Piccadilly, London

حمیر کو دعا، علی اور عدیل کو بہت سا پیار۔ ان سے پوچھ لو کہ لندن سے انہیں کیا چاہیئے۔

ابو

003/79

ماسکو
۲۳ جولائی

پیاری میزو،

بہت دنوں کے بعد تمہارا خط ملا، بہت مسرت ہوئی، خاص طور سے اس خبر سے
کہ آخر تمہاری آزمائش ختم ہوئی اور تمہیں اپنی مرضی کا کام بھی مل گیا۔ اب اس نے
ہونا، اس کے بعد سے گھر بنانے کا دردِ سر، لڑکے بھیجے جائیں اور پھر چھوٹی موٹی بات
پر پریشان ہوتی ہو۔ لیکن مزاج تو کوئی بدل نہیں سکتا پھر بھی ان کی کوشش کرے
تو کچھ تھوڑا بہت تو عقل سے کام لے ہی سکتا ہے اور عقل کا تقاضا ہے کہ محض پریشان
ہونے سے تو کوئی مسئلہ حل نہیں ہو سکتا۔ بہتر یہی ہے کہ جب کوئی پریشانی کا مضمون پیدا
ہو تو اسے دور کرنے کی کوشش کرو۔ ہم ساتھ ہی ان کی کچھ Scotch Art بھی آزما
کہ جو چیز کھو جاتی ہے اور ڈھونڈنے سے کیا فائدہ۔ اپنا نسخہ تو یہ ہے جو ہم بہت دفعہ
میں بھی استعمال کرتے رہے کہ جب ہم گھر کی آواز زیادہ قریب سے آنے لگتی تو ہم
منہ سر لپیٹ کر سو جاتے تھے۔ ہمارے ساتھی حسن لیسو آکر پوچھتے تھے کہ تم
اتنے شور میں سو کیسے جاتے ہو؟ ہم نے بتایا کہ ان کے آنے سے پہلے دماغ پر زور ڈال
یعنی will power کو کام میں لا کر کچھ بھی نقصان نہ ہو تو کیسے کچھ حد تک کام ہو ہی
جاتا ہے، ضد جیسے کام ہو تو پھر بھی ہنسی آ جاتا، کاہلی اب برسات کے بعد ہی شروع
کرو تو اچھا ہے تاکہ ہم بھی گھر پہنچ جائیں، کیونکہ تمہاری امی نے دھمکی دی ہے کہ جب تک گھر بننے کا

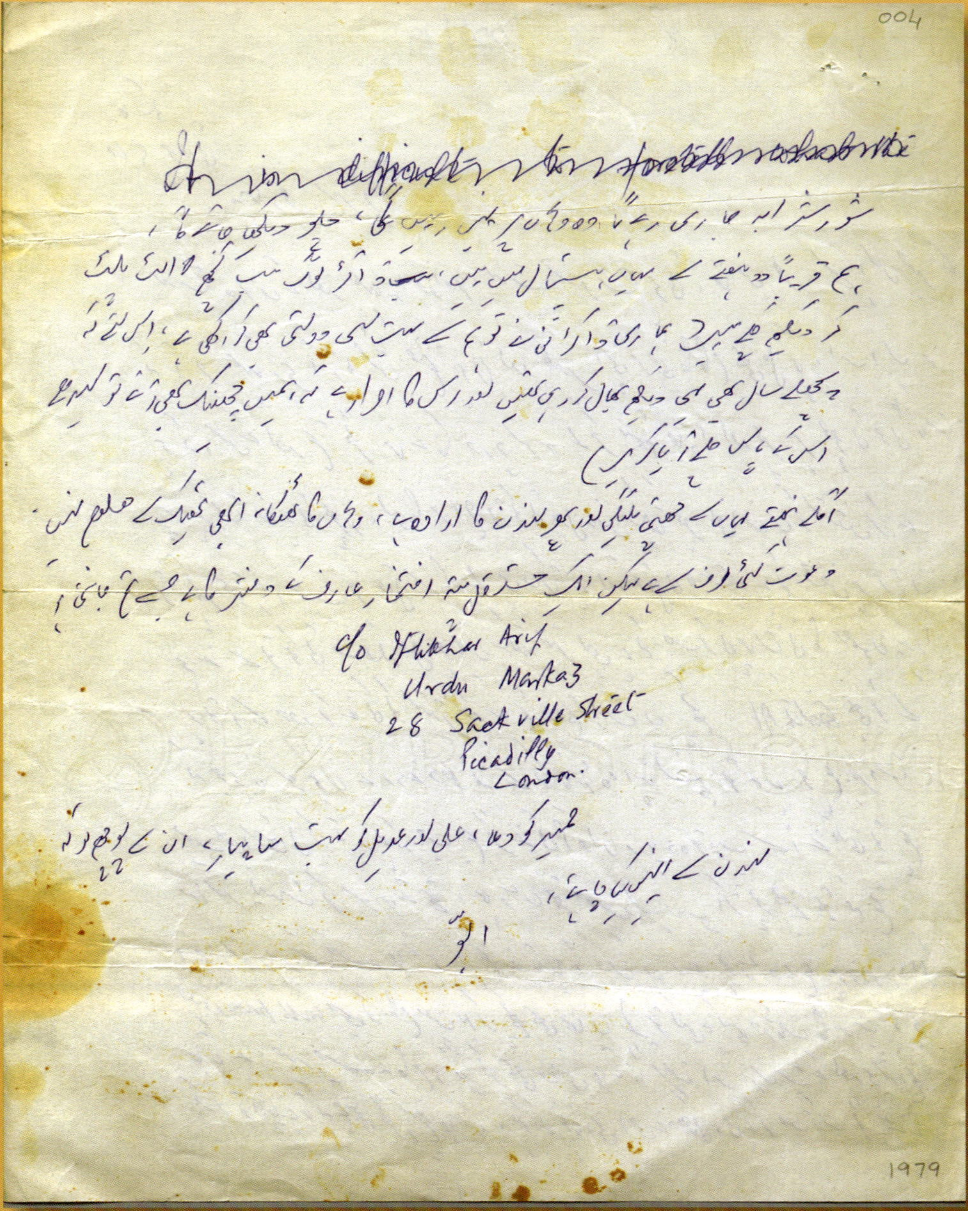

004

~~[illegible] difficult [illegible]~~

شور شرابہ ہماری [illegible] ۵۰۰۰ [illegible] پہنچ گئی، چلو دیکھیں [illegible]

آج قریب دو ہفتے کے بعد ہسپتال سے ہمیں رخصت [illegible] سب [illegible] الحمد للہ

تو دیکھیں گے ہماری [illegible] قوم کے بہت لوگ [illegible] اس لئے

پچھلے سال بھی یہی [illegible] نہ ہمیں [illegible]

اس کے پاس چلے آ جائیں گی

اگلے ہفتے یہاں سے چھٹی ملنے پر لندن کا ارادہ ہے، وہاں کا ٹھکانہ ابھی ٹھیک سے معلوم نہیں

[illegible] ایک [illegible] افتخار عارف کے دفتر کا پتہ بھیج رہا ہوں

C/o Iftikhar Arif
Urdu Markaz
28 Sackville Street
Piccadilly
London.

منیزہ کو دعا، علی اور عدیل کو بہت سا پیار، ان سے پوچھو کہ لندن سے کیا منگوانا چاہتے ہیں

ابو

1979

My trendsetter accomplishments

Although you were never one to blow your own trumpet, there was always a smug grin on your face when you knew you had hit home with a poem, or some good deed you had just helped happen. Never did I hear you say anything or have a look that spelt any arrogance. I heard so many stories about your having helped so many people by making a phone call or even a visit on their behalf, or writing letters of recommendation for them which later shaped their lives in a positive way. And when someone thanked you or fell over backwards trying to praise you or show their gratitude, you would always smile and say, "Bhai hum nay aik phone hi kiya tha" (we merely made a phone call). So, maybe, that is what I will also say here, "Bhai hum nay to aik programme hi kiya tha" (we merely did a programme). But then those programmes went on to become trendsetters, and are still, many, many years later, talked about as milestones in the programming history of PTV.

Now that I look back I must have directed hundreds or maybe thousands of programmes in the forty plus years I was in PTV. And I helped create so many more programmes or brainstormed about them with their producers.

So many governments came and went during those years, so many Ministers,
Secretaries of Information, Managing Directors and Chairmen that I cannot even recall all of them. So many directives and counter-directives were issued during those years telling us how to conduct ourselves, how to address each other, how to ensure that our talent on screen looked "decent". We even had a clock-in and clock-out machine fitted at the entrance to PTV Lahore Station once. We had small windows cut into the doors of the producers' rooms to make sure no hanky panky business went on behind those doors (as if doors stopped anybody at any time from getting up to antics). I promptly covered the window in my room with paper and insisted that as a female I would not allow anyone to peek in whenever they felt like it. It was resisted by the management at the time, but I stood my ground. They would take it off. I would put it on again. After a few weeks they gave up. Obviously!

I think the only Minister worth mentioning here is Javed Jabbar. He was funny, bordering on sarcasm. I recall a conversation I had with him one morning as he was driving to the National Assembly, to answer a question about a drama of Lahore PTV, in which a young Christian girl, who had converted to Islam, had walked out of her 'Muslim' in-laws' house because of their taunts and ill treatment. The mullahs were up in arms about it. I told JJ the girl had used her right to choose her own path. She had not given up on Islam but on the torture of the in-laws and their constant jibes about her conversion. She was standing up for her rights. He agreed and said, "I knew you would bring in that angle. Ok. I get the picture." I did not hear any complaints about that series after that.

On the Managing Director front it was and would be only Aslam Azhar who stood out head and shoulders above all others. He had his blind spots, but he listened and gave you space.

I was talking about my forty years and what I can proudly fall back on as my contribution to PTV which now unfortunately has become, what some people would say, a channel to switch off.

Let me start by telling you about the setting up of an hour's programme called 'Khawateen Time' on PTV, meant for women.
The opposition I faced from the management at the time was certainly my biggest challenge.

It took me months of persuasion to convince them that I was only asking for one hour in the morning, which was anyway a non-productive commercial time. I was not asking for too many funds nor for extra staff. And I sold the idea on the fact that PTV would be the only channel at the time to dedicate a special hour of programming for women in South Asia. That argument probably appealed all the officers, as they probably saw it as an opportunity to push their own profiles in the corridors of power. I was new at the game at the time. Having just been persuaded to take over the General Managership of PTV Lahore, I was also out to make a mark for myself but my objective was not myself but my audience, especially the women viewers. And if I got some of the stardust sprinkled on me in the process, well, why not.

Khawateen Time was finally launched, only for an hour every day, with Sundays off.

I don't clearly recall when this special transmission started taking off, both commercially and viewership-wise, when did the dedicated team begin to get formed, when did new ideas start happening, when did audience responses start shaping the content. But it happened organically, and I just went with the flow.
Two incidents stand out clearly in my mind.

The first: I went to see my favourite person, the late Bano Qudsia, to ask her to participate in one of the programmes.
"No," she said. I was slightly taken aback. Bhabi, as I had known her for years, was not a 'no' kind of person.
"Because I will not be a part of a zenana daba (a female only compartment), she said.
That was food for thought for me. Was I trying to create a separate space for the women audiences only? Was I falling into the same trap as all feminists are accused of? "We want our space. Everyone else move out" Was I even clear about where I was headed?

To this day I am grateful to Bano Apa for helping me clarify my objectives about where I was headed with this initiative.

I would not create a separate utopia for a female audience only. I would not make a 'zenana daba'. I first of all had to identify that special segment of audience which existed with perhaps different tastes and focus than the general group of viewers and deserved to have their needs and wishes fulfilled. At the same time I should not be completely isolating other audiences. Here is the formula I came up with.
Dramas for all age groups, but with a focus on gender issues.

Talk shows with both male and female participants, with the focus on gender sensitization.

Cookery programmes, home décor programmes, gardening programmes, child care programmes, but never was it said or implied that only females should be watching them. The programmes were gender neutral in their approach, I made certain of that.

The second vivid memory I have is of the Khwateen Time all day transmissions we would have on March 8th was to celebrate International Women's Day. That day, the entire PTV station would be decorated elaborately. We would plan for weeks ahead. The entire premises would be swarming with visitors of all ages, dressed colourfully, chatting away. Laughter would be heard all over the building. A raffle would be held of old electric appliances that had been sitting in the basement for years, rotting away. They were put in order and sent off with the enthusiastic winners. The evening entertainment shows were absolutely amazing. All top performers of music and comedy participated before hundreds of bubbly and energetic youngsters, who would sway and clap with the music for hours on end. However, that day the participants would be restricted to females only. What celebrations we had! Music blared well into the evening, and everyone including my team and crew went home those evenings, exhausted but satisfied.

I would call this transmission a trendsetter, because once the private channels started happening, each and every one of them started the morning transmissions fairly much on the same pattern as Khawateen Time. What I observed was that no guidance went into the content planning. I have heard that marriage proposals were being discussed on air, which I feel were setting rather low standards: Mehndi designs at Eid time; how to sew fancy joras for parties; make-up and hair styles for weddings and parties; quiz shows in which gifts were thrown away and people in the audience could be seen scrambling all over themselves, to collect a cooker or a fan or a hamper of sweets. The questions asked were of an equally low standard: how many times does your mother-in-law scold you in a day or your husband smiles at you. This on-going practice has reduced the intelligence of the tele-viewers to just above that of a guinea pig, especially when we examine the existing social environment and its background. It made me shudder when I heard about these shows and how the audience would squeal and whistle their approval. No wonder there are long queues of people trying to get passes to enter this horrendous show. Actually, the audiences themselves cannot be absolved either from being used in this cheap and indiscriminate manner. But I digress as usual from what I was telling you.

So yes, that was a programme series I have been enriched by.
I can also actually say that I have been responsible for placing the term "gender" on the map of PTV.

Well, you never had to do that because it was really not your style. For you, it was always a smile, a gesture, and of course your verses which said it all. But I guess in this matter I took after Mama, who never minced her words and said it like it was and up front. In fact, multiple times I have been reprimanded by Ali or even Adeel to behave more like you than Mama. A polite way of telling me to be more diplomatic. I don't like sugar-coating my words and diluting what I mean. It goes against my nature. One aspect of this transmission, which I think again broke the set norms and made waves, was when I decided (and fought for it) that it should go live, with questions posed to professionals while sitting in the studio. Live programming had been discontinued on PTV years earlier. It was, I suppose, in continuing the policy to gag the freedom of speech by Zia ul Haq. The ban just stayed in place, for the fear of someone airing their views, which could be in direct clash with the establishment of that time. I had to put up the argument that I was reaching out to women, who were less threatening than men, in airing their views, and probably less violent in their use of language, etc. I really made up quite a tale of defence. Then came the logistics of it. Two telephone lines were especially sanctioned, to be set up in a small ante-room next to the control room where I would sit and do the live production. Those telephone numbers would be widely circulated, through Khwateen Time, for public consumption. Two members of my production crew would man those numbers during the Friday morning session. We called it Khwateen Time On line.

Callers would give their name and question, which the apprentice producer would write down, and a runner would bring it to me. I would take just a few seconds to review it for any questionable content, and once approved, the same runner would dash down to the studio and hand it over to the moderator, who would then read it out for the viewers as well as the person who was the guest that morning. The runner would then rush back and take the next question, and this 'relay' race would go on for the next hour until we closed the show. There were so many angles to focus on: the question, its language, the possible answer whether it was 'safe' to ask it live, the toing and froing of the runners, ensuring they were never seen on camera as they darted in and out of the studio, up the stairs, down the stairs, hand over, takeover, etc. And at the same time, I had to be vigilant throughout, watching the studio, reading the questions, shouting directions to the cameramen, looking at the clock. It used to be quite a circus on Fridays I recall, but exciting and so full of energy, since everyone was on their toes.

There were some people who were much more popular than others. Medical guests had many questions; legal guests had so much to answer; celebs who were with their guards down were bombarded with queries. And the phones kept ringing long after the show was over, with many complaining that they had not been able to get through, which was probably quite true. Those were not the days of mobile phones, so we were all at the mercy of PTCL throughout.

One particularly funny session (perhaps not funny, but an eye opener for me that has stayed with me all these years) was the first one conducted with Dr Khalida Usmani, the breast cancer specialist, who I had, and still have, the highest regard for. She was forthcoming, open-minded, direct. Perhaps I found similarities with her approach to my own. We became good friends and I took the plunge of inviting her to the live show. She was most accommodating because she felt the issue of breast cancer needed so much more explanation and awareness-raising.

As she was being 'puffed', as we call it in the make-up room, I suddenly had a sinking feeling. "Dr Sahiba. How are we going to handle this conversation? I mean ...." And here I floundered. How do you call a breast a breast on national network and that too on a live broadcast? She understood my discomfort. "How about I discuss 'chathi ka cancer' and talk about the 'inner clothes' which have to be of cotton instead of calling them underwear or brassieres? I will call them the 'inner small clothes' and any female listening should be able to grasp what I mean". With just ten minutes to go live, that was the best solution I could think of.

Dr. Khalida Usmani in Tum Jo Chaho Tu Suno, PTV Lahore

I remember clearly, thinking, as I was putting on my head phones in the control room, "Well this is either a make or break programme. You are going to be branded as vulgar, propagating obscenity on PTV, talking about hugely taboo parts of the body, about underwear and brassieres, even though it will be in coded language. Get ready." It was two minutes to air time. The phones had started ringing. My guest was being wired. My anchor was loosening up her shoulders a bit and I was saying a short prayer of getting through the ordeal smoothly. "Stand by studio. Thirty seconds to live." I heard my floor manager shout. The title was on air and we started
transmission. "Cut to camera two," I said and the moderator began the introduction of Dr Khalida Usmani. This could perhaps have been one of my most challenging but most rewarding presentations. Doctor Sahiba (RIP) was a champion to the cause of creating awareness about breast cancer. An excellent speaker, she diplomatically handled every question deftly, and they were flowing in and out of the studio fast. As we sat down for a well-earned cup of tea later in my office Dr Khalida paid me a compliment which I hold dear to my heart even today, after more than twenty years. "Moneeza, you might have saved many young women today from providing them this information. Breast cancer is a menace which is hidden under taboos and shame. You have opened that door today for many young women." Whether we did that or not, it was a huge tribute from one of this country's finest medical minds. I mourned her passing deeply.

So, onto my next, what I term a trendsetter, production.
It was many, many years ago when PTV was black-and-white and we had limited transmission hours and Monday was the weekly off when I got hooked onto an interview programme titled 'Face to Face'. It was from an American channel and aired on PTV. In those days, PTV had regular English programme slots. Films, comedy shows, cartoons and this interview series. I still remember the interview I saw was of King Hussain of Jordan. What intrigued me was not the interview itself, but the manner of questioning of the interviewer. The questions were short and focused, to get the best out of the person seated in front of him. And if that person happened to be a monarch in his own right, well, then you had to be generally on your toes anyway. But there was no grovelling or bending over flattery. The interviewer, John Freeman, was keeping to all protocols of facing royalty, without stooping too low or being over presumptuous. King Hussain too was a good speaker, and the programme was a treat to watch. It must have stayed locked away somewhere in the corners of my mind for years.

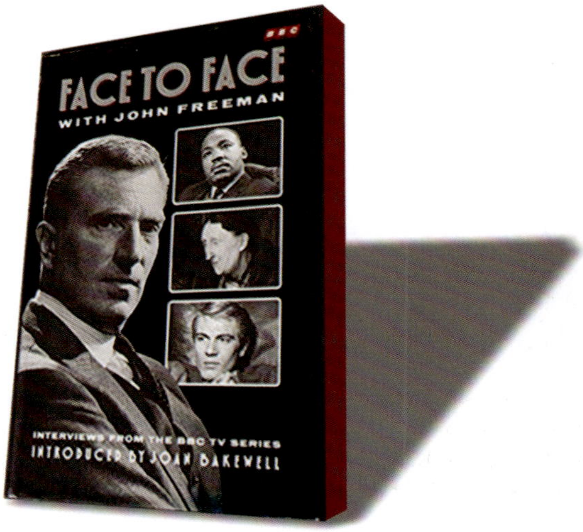

Until one day, quite out of the blue, the idea came to me of doing such a programme myself. What brought on this thought escapes me, but I started chewing on it. In those days and we are talking early nineties, it was not PTV policy to allow any regular employee to appear on screen. In fact it was positively discouraged. And if now and then someone did have to come on screen, they would receive no payment for their toils. So my first battle was to persuade the PTV management of allowing me to be the moderator of this interview programme. It was the rule at the time to produce a pilot programme, put it up for approval at the General Manager conference for it to be critiqued, either praised or torn to bits by the 'rivalries' that went on between different centres. Lahore vs Karachi centre was the main battle ground. It was all very subtle, very politely done. But all so obvious. When I took over as GM Lahore, I fought each battle up front, loud and clear without mincing words. I would go for the jugular every time. You know me, right? It was very obvious to me that there were underlying gender issues at play as well. First of all, how dare a female enter this sacred space of management? Then a female who is competent and confident as well; then someone who spoke her mind and defended her Centre with such clarity; then someone who would not cow down and be out-argued; then someone who would find alternatives and options as the conversation flowed and who would give solutions as the discussions progressed. I made so many petty enemies during those years when I was General Manager. The longest GM to hold office to date I may proudly add. But I also learnt to side step the mines and tap dance all the way. And that also caused much agony. Anyway, so there I was one day with my pilot, featuring Uzma Gillani, the versatile drama actor, talking about her personal and professional life. The set was a dream, uncluttered and beautifully lit and the camera shots were amazing. But guess what? The tele audience did not see my face once! That was my tactic of side-stepping the criticism I knew would come. Throughout the interview the camera was on Uzma. Even as she listened to my questions, we caught her every twitch, every gesture, every eye movement, the shifting of her feet and hands. And even those movements spoke volumes. I also made another interesting change. I wore white and only white so as to again enhance the presence of the guest. Well, surprisingly, both these changes were appreciated by the people around the table and the programme series was approved. It was titled Tum Jo Chaho Tau Suno . Based on one of your verses, sung by Tina Sani, this series went on to record more than a hundred programmes. I met so many brilliant people. I interviewed so many giants of their fields. I travelled across the country for recordings. And I kept getting asked, "Why can't we see you?" And I would smile and say "This was not about me, but my guest". I did so enjoy these programmes and the privilege of meeting some people who I would never otherwise have been able to reach. Naseem Wali Khan. Gulgee. Hanif Khan. Dr Ruth Pfau. Dr Qadeer. Benazir Bhutto. Bilquis Edhi. The list is endless and my life is all the more richer for documenting these icons for posterity. Of course, most of them would start the conversation about you and your poetry while we were being wired-up. Some shared memories of meeting you, some spoke about their experiences with you and so on. It helped ease the tension. I must admit, there were times when I felt a bit of a fraud, luring them to the studio using leverage of your name, but when they sat before me and the cameras started rolling, then it was just me and them as I probed their past, asked them to share their future dreams and frustrations facing their present. Rarely did I come out of an interview without my guest praising my way of handling the

This programme series is now being broadcast on my YouTube Channel 'Moneeza Hashmi kay Sath' and is receiving much accolade.

questions and allowing them to speak at length. And that includes Benazir Bhutto, who shared some interesting aspects of her life with Asif Zardari. I was amused at some of her comments, which had to be edited out for obvious reasons. My interview with Imran Khan was also an interesting one. As he took the microphone off, he told me he had never been asked such questions before.

Justice Fakhrunisa in Tum Jo Chaho Tu Suno, PTV Lahore

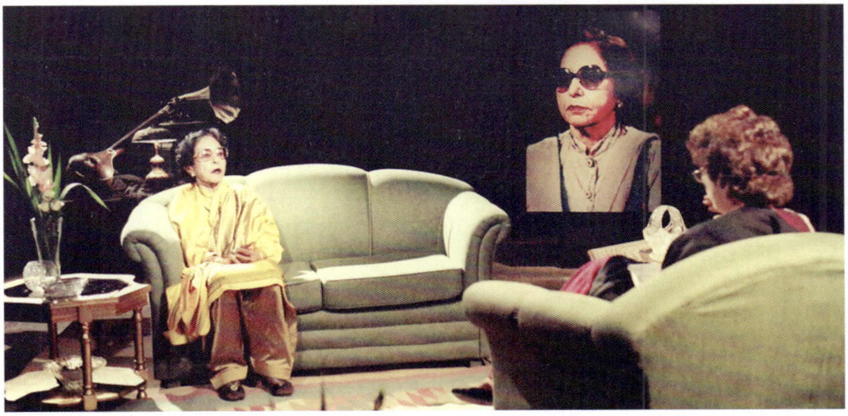

Malika Pukhraj in Tum Jo Chaho Tu Suno, PTV Lahore

Frankly, that was a compliment because I had had only a few hours to set up the interview so there was no research there, just thinking on my feet… Some people I could not nail down, and for that I feel truly sorry. I did give it my best, but they were either elusive or the timing was not right or our stars were not aligned. Well, there is still time.

I also did so many other programmes over these forty plus years. For children, for young people, for women, talk shows, magazine programmes, interview shows, docu-dramas, etc., but I did not attempt directing drama at any time. I wonder why, now. Drama always gets the most ratings. It gets you the most so-called 'fame', short-lived as it may be. It gets you awards. It gets you media and press hype. You make contacts with the celebs. It kind of 'makes you for life'. But somehow I always felt it was not one's own creation. It was written by someone else, the words were spoken by others, and all you, as a director, were responsible for were the camera shots, the lighting and the editing. Even the casting was done by others. It could be someone who would bring in the commercial breaks, or generally, who could make your life miserable.

I, as you will know, always wanted it my own way. I carved my own path wherever it would take me. There have been times when I have regretted speaking out as candidly as I did and suffered the consequences. But at the end of the day, I lived my life by my own rules, so I guess I am responsible for the successes (few) and failures (plenty) in life, but at least I sleep with my own conscience at night, without any burdens. I do the burning and cribbing, but not about my own decisions.

So, drama has never been my forte, but I did try my hand with music programmes once and I must say that it was a positive experience and it was not a flop either as I had thought it might be. I had been again inspired by another show I had seen somewhere (maybe on Sony) and decided to do an experiment.

For no reason except on a whim, I called it 'Melody Night'. I selected all the top singers of the country and got them to sing oldies and golden era songs in each programme, which brought in the composers we had forgotten about, but whose melodies still were so unforgettable that they have stayed alive. Khursheed Anwar, Khalil Ahmad, Robin Ghosh, Hasan Latif, Master Nazar, and so on. I made it into a sort of club atmosphere, with the singer perched on a high stool. The orchestra were all dressed in black, performing live (or so it appeared to the viewer), and each and every number was selected by me and my team. I could not actually shoot this programme myself, as my understanding of moving cameras on a musical beat was not up to the mark, so my friend and colleague Ayub Khawar stepped in and took over. He was the 'Studio Director' and I was the 'Selective Director'. We brought back dozens and dozens of great music items, long forgotten in time, sung by Madam Noor Jahan, Naseem Begum, Mala, Runa Laila, Mehnaz, Zubaida Khanum, Kausar Parveen and others. Mehdi Hasan and Ahmad Rushdi were the male favourites we chose from along with Saleem Raza and Habib Wali Mohammad. The programme was a joy to plan, and then listening to the comments of the singers who had such a great time recording these items, was a delight. As you know, great music never dies and music is food for the soul. It can move you to another level of spirituality, where one can feel one's inner self floating with the universe. Imagine enjoying that feeling of weightlessness as one glides with the melody! It is the same with any art form. No one would know this feeling better than you.

Well, enough of my achievements!
You know, as one grows older, things can happen two ways.
Either you feel you have been there, seen it, done it and now need your privacy. And a 'leave me alone' strategy comes into place.

Or you can hear the clock ticking, the body creaking, the legs trembling, the eyes blurring, the mind forgetting, so you want to have as much of the centre stage as possible.
Talking about myself, now at the age of seventy five I think I'm done. I shy away from cameras. Frankly, I just feel its bad taste to keep projecting oneself and thrusting oneself forward. Shall I tell you a secret? All I ever felt elated about was to see my name at the end of my programmes on PTV and still revel in it.

Inside, I would pinch myself and say well done, now let's move on.
And as I am stepping into my declining years (sometimes fast, sometimes slow), I really, want to just sit back and savour my thoughts on what I did achieve (if anything). There are times when I sit on my sofa in my room and look out of the window and see images of so many memories dancing before my eyes. I capture one thought and then play with it. How, when, with whom, what happened and so on. It has become quite a relaxing past time and I often find myself yearning to sit and dwell on the past. At times there is a pull at my heart to meet those friends again. At times, the laughter of that moment rings clearly in my ears and often a thought brings tears to my eyes, and I let them roll down my cheeks as a tribute to that

moment. And then it's time to move on---

When I look at the photographs taken after you recovered from your 'near death' experience in February 1984, I get the same feeling. As if you knew it was only a matter of time now. You look weaker, a sort of 'settled', as if you are waiting for the final curtain. That photo of you with Ustaad Daman so clearly depicts that.

Faiz and Ustad Daman, Lahore 1984

Then, your visit to the village on 19 November 1984, praying at the village mosque, meeting your relatives there, then going onto Jassar, your mother Bebe ji's village to meet more relatives seems to be a premonition of it being your last visit. And as it happened it turned out to be almost your last day on earth…

That look on your face as you were gasping on 20th November, 1984 in Mayo Hospital has stayed with me all these years, and will still be with me probably until I take my last breath. Your colour had turned a pale green. You were sitting up struggling for breath. Your body slumped. I screamed out for a doctor as I leapt to hold you. Dr Javed Gardezi, who was the house doctor at the time, raced in and told me to leave the room in no uncertain terms. I stumbled out and sat on a bench close by. Nurses and doctors started running into the room. Medical equipment was brought. My mind closed down for those few minutes. The hospital corridor continued its business. People streaming this way and that. Sounds of chattering and then the sound of the Zuhur Azaan.
I waited …
A few minutes later, Dr Gardezi came out. His facial expression said it all.
It was time to bid you a final good bye.

Letter

004 / 79
Ayot Place, Ayot St Peters
Welwyn Herts, London
18 /8

Dear Mizu,

Received your letter. I was happy to hear that you are satisfied with your job and that you are also handling some other assignments. I believe that if the job is to one's taste and it does not require more effort than one's energies and capacities then well and good, otherwise it does not make for good sense to stress yourself out. The construction of your house has started…congratulations. It won't be completed by the time we come but some sort of a shape would have evolved. Your savings of a lakh-and-half would have been used up in that but by then more money will be arranged. There is no need to fret about that as yet. You have written about your Ammee. Actually the thing is that because of loneliness and overwork she needs some pampering and support. Whenever you people have the time, do go and see her. Things will sort themselves out once I am back.

Now for my doings… most of the time is spent in this huge palace and beautiful garden far from London. Watched the Test match on television. Whatever may be Pakistan's condition, but at least it has made it in cricket and so the people must be exhilarated. Sometimes after a break of three, four days I go to London to spend the evening. The other day I got to listen to Asad Amanat Ali sing. Tomorrow or the day after I shall preside over a function and then next week there is a longish television interview to be done. So, I am comfortable. There are invitations from Amsterdam, Stockholm, Canada, Iran, etc., and then in October after dealing with all these I have to return home.

Till then, Khuda Hafiz and love to everyone.
Abbu

خط

004 / 79
Ayot Place, Ayot St Peters
Welwyn Herts, London
18 /8

پیاری میزو

تمہارا خط ملا۔ یہ سن کر خوشی ہوئی کہ اب تم اپنی ملازمت سے مطمئن ہو اور اس کے علاوہ کچھ اور کام بھی سنبھال رکھا ہے۔ صرف اتنا ہے کہ اگر کام اپنی پسند کا ہو اور اس میں اپنی سکت اور بساط سے زیادہ محنت درکار نہ ہو تو ٹھیک ہے ورنہ محض پیسے کی خاطر اپنے آپ کو ہلکان کرنا دانشمندی کی بات نہیں۔ تمہارے مکان کی تعمیر شروع ہو گئی۔ مبارک ہو۔ ہمارے آنے تک تو خیر یہ کیسے ختم ہو سکتی ہے لیکن اس کی کچھ صورت تو نکل آئے گی۔ جب تک تمہارا لاکھ ڈیڑھ لاکھ خرچ ہو گا تب مزید پیسے بھی کہیں سے آ جائیں گے۔ ابھی سے اس بارے میں فکر کرنے کی ضرورت نہیں۔ تم نے اپنی امی کے بارے میں لکھا ہے۔ بات صرف اتنی ہے کہ آج کل انہیں تنہائی اور مصروفیت کے باعث کچھ ناز برداری اور دلجوئی کی ضرورت رہتی ہے۔ جب بھی تم لوگوں کو کچھ وقت ملے ان سے مل آیا کرو۔ جب ہم آ جائیں گے تو سب ٹھیک ہو جائے گا۔

اپنا احوال یہ ہے کہ لندن سے دور اس بہت بڑے محل اور خوبصورت باغ میں زیادہ وقت گزرتا ہے۔ TV پہ Test Match دیکھا۔ پاکستان کا اور تو جیسا حال ہے سو ہے لیکن کم از کم کرکٹ ہی میں میدان مار لیا جس سے ظاہر ہے کہ لوگ باغ باغ ہو گئے ہوں گے۔ دوسرے چوتھے دن کبھی شام گزارنے لندن چلے جاتے ہیں۔ اگلے دن اسد امانت علی کا گانا سنا، کل پرسوں ایک تقریب کی صدارت کریں گے اور اگلے ہفتے T.V پر ایک طویل انٹرویو کرنا ہے۔ غرض آرام سے گزرتی ہے۔ پھر امسٹرڈم، سٹاک ہالم، کینیڈا، ایران وغیرہ سے دعوت نامے ہیں اور اکتوبر میں یہ سب کچھ نبٹا کر گھر لوٹ آئیں گے۔

جب تک خدا حافظ اور سب کو بہت سا پیار۔

ابو

004/79

Ayot Place
Ayot St Peters
~~Welwyn~~
Welwyn
Herts
18/8

پیاری منیزہ، تمہارا خط ملا،

یہ سن کر خوشی ہوئی کہ اب تم اپنی ملازمت سے
مطمئن ہو اور اس کے علاوہ کچھ اور کام بھی سنبھال
رکھے ہیں۔ صرف اتنا ہے کہ اگر کام اپنی پسند کا ہو اور
اس میں اپنی صلاحیت لڑانے سے زیادہ محنت
درکار نہ ہو تو ٹھیک ہے ورنہ محض پیسے کی خاطر
اپنے آپ کو ہلکان کرنا دانشمندی کی بات نہیں۔
تمہارے مکان کی تعمیر شروع ہو گئی، مبارک ہو۔ ہمارے
آنے تک تو شاید یہ کام ختم ہو سکتا ہے لیکن اس کی
کچھ صورت تو نکل آئے گی، جب تک تمہارا ایک لاکھ
ڈیڑھ لاکھ خرچ ہو گا جب تک مزید پیسے کہیں
سے نہ مل جائیں گے۔ ابھی سے اس بارے میں فکر کرنے کی
ضرورت نہیں۔ تم نے اپنی امی کے بارے میں لکھا ہے،
بات صرف اتنی ہے کہ آج کل انہیں تنہائی اور [illegible]

005

ہے بہت کچھ نازبرداری اور دیکھ بھال کی ضرورت ہے۔
جب کبھی تم لوگوں کو کچھ وقت ملے ان سے مل آیا کرو۔ جب
ہم آجائیں گے تو سب ٹھیک ہو جائے گا۔

اپنا احوال یہ ہے کہ لندن کے دور ایک بہت بڑے محل
اور خوبصورت باغ میں زیادہ وقت گزرتا ہے۔ ۲۷ کو
Test Match دیکھنے جاؤں گا اور تو جیسا ملا ہے کوئی لیکن
کم از کم کرکٹ کی میدان ہو یا جس کے ظاہر ہے کہ لوگ
پانچ پانچ دن کھیلتے رہیں گے۔ دوسرے چوتھے دن کبھی تو گزرا
لندن چلے جاتے ہیں۔ اگلے دن والدہ بنت علی خانم نانا نے کل پر یوں
اکسلوژیب سے ملاقات کرینگے اور اگلے ہفتے ۱۷ اگست
ہموطن انشورنس کو ہوتا ہے۔ غرض آج کل گزرتی ہے۔ میرا مشورہ
مشتاق کی طرح کینیڈا امریکہ وغیرہ سے دعوت نامے آئے ہیں لیکن
انکو رد کردیا ہے۔ سب کچھ بتانا ہو تو وقت آ جائے گا۔
جب تک ہم ... خدا حافظ اور سب کو بہت سا پیار۔
ابو

1979

My spiritual journey and your part in it

I cannot exactly recall when you made the following remark. I wanted to take you with me to Data Sahib's for a "haazri" and you laughingly said, "She will ask forgiveness for all of our sins." And you guffawed loudly..
I don't recall if you did go with me that day or not but somehow intuitively you could see my tilt (or whatever you want to call it) towards being spiritually inclined, which no one else in the family was.
How odd is that, I sometimes wonder.

Could it be Bebeji's influence? She never ever spoke to us about saying our prayers or doing this or that religious activity, but perhaps watching her twirl her prayer beads with a simple smile on her face, lost in a world of her own, lips silently moving, a black skull cup covered with a white cotton chadder, chewing her naswar off and on, dressed always in a simple cotton shalwar kameez, feet in black open chappals, always a musty smell around her (which could have been a mixture of the naswar and just plainly the fragrance of a clean body which was rigorously washed five times a day at least). She was my friend, if you can understand that. I would rag and tease her no end, put on her black burqa and go prancing around the house, much to her amusement and at times annoyance. I would distract her while she was praying simply to amuse myself! I watch my grandchildren creep out of the room if they see me praying and wonder how I could have been so heartless to this harmless and gentle old soul.

Aunty Bali and us!

But despite it all, I do think I imbibed her strong sense of faith at a subconscious level, which has steered me along many a rocky path in my life.

Then there was Aunty Bali. Iqbal Begum, as she is known in public, but to me she was another life-line.

Aunty Bali, who you were also extremely attached to, even though she was only your half sister, became my mentor and confidante after you departed. Her very gentle persona also became a familiar sight to all my friends when they came to my house for milads or aftaaris. She would sit in one corner and greet all of them by name. I tried my best to look after her for as long as I could. I would tease her just as I did Bebeji but loved visiting her in Icchra to eat something she had cooked for me, or hear the latest gossip about a family member, or listen to her talk about my childhood capers and so on and so forth. Adeel also went to her for Maths tuition for his Matric exams, and she always had peas "pillau" and "aloo gosht" ready for him. She sent me home-made recipes for Hamzah when I went to the USA, and she made herbal tonics for Ali's children. She was special to the core and also religious.

So I think my so-called spirituality is 'their' fault, indirectly, but I accept it with a huge sense of gratitude.

In these, my waning years, when I get lost for a sense of direction or afraid of where I will finally land up after my breath ceases, the strong faith in the Divine bequeathed to me by these two special women keeps me moving ahead in finding hope and courage.

And this journey has taken me to some interesting places of which some are off the beaten path.

I want to tell you about those places and those journeys.

So where do I begin?

It should be with Haj I guess.
There are times when I get sucked into situations that take over my life. Did you ever experience that? You know when matters just start rolling and the tide takes you with it. Even if you want to, there is no way to go the opposite route. You go with the flow as it were. The same thing happened with me in 2004.

I remember a remark by Mrs Mustansar Hussain Tarrar at a dinner which stuck in my head. The couple had returned from Haj and she remarked, "If you want to make this journey, make sure your son accompanies you."

When the actual idea of Haj somehow started making the rounds in and around me, the first person I turned to was Adeel. He had recently got married and I wasn't sure if I was encroaching on his private life. He asked only one question, "For how long?" "Three weeks," I replied. He agreed and the forms started being filled up. We were four in that group. Adeel, our mehram, Nadia, Aunty Bali's daughter and a close friend, Huma. We got into the quota and off we went on this arduous and somewhat uncomfortable journey. There are so many stories about those three weeks which would bore you and are terribly lengthy to tell. Like, when we land at Jeddah on a cold early morning and wait, hungry and tired for five hours or more for the clearances, with thousands of people milling around creating a chaotic environment. The hotel room was shared by all of us, as was the bathroom. Then the poor old lady whose wallet got stolen, and we looked out for her throughout our stay in Mina, especially at meal times. The endless traffic jams, getting to and from anywhere. The head and shoulders pushing and pulling while performing tawaaf. The queues outside the bathrooms. The need to sleep which completely evaded us, until we

landed in Madina after ten days. The day when Adeel was nearly crushed in the stampede that happened that year at the place where the devils are stoned (Jumrat), was perhaps the worst day of my life. Since I did not go for that particular ritual, I heard the news of the stampede on TV in my hotel room and thought my heart had stopped beating. The utter and absolute panic of those few hours is a thought that still makes me take deep breaths. I remember thinking: "Where on earth do I go looking for him?" I also recall screaming in my head to Allah asking Him to intervene. "Why did You do this? Why?" I kept asking, tears rolling down my face. Suddenly I felt suffocated in that hotel room. I told Huma I had to go to the Kaaba and pray there. He will listen. He has to. He is the All Merciful Allah. He cannot let this happen. We raced down the stairs and there, to my utter relief, I saw Adeel walk into the hotel. His face was ashen, his steps faltering, his clothes messed up. But he was alive. My prayers had been heard. Huma held my arm as my legs gave way. The story Adeel told of the stampede came out days later. He was silent for a couple of days, shaken, traumatized and unnerved. But alive.
Yes, that memory will stay with me till the day I die.

Madina was a breeze. We all coughed and sneezed and choked with the multitude of viruses floating around, but we made it home in one piece.
I visited Ajmer Shareef twice, but both times it was a somewhat quiet experience.
First of all, we stand out as Pakistani Muslims, and the people who claim to be the caretakers of the shrine are on the lookout for pilgrims like us that they can coerce and sometimes bully into giving them more money. I guess you have these types everywhere. So in the efforts to avoid them, the actual spirituality of my experience was dissipated. I wanted to talk to the Saint. I wanted to share my thoughts with him. I wanted to feel his presence within me. But both times my visit became a ritual of paying my respects and trying to silence the cries of beggars around me and demands on my wallet. But I did feel better, no doubt for having been there, and saying my nawafil (prayers) in his presence.

Nizam ud Din Aulia's shrine in Delhi was exactly the same, if not worse. The approach is dirty and noisy. The incense perfume makes one heady and almost giddy. The constant touching and wails of the beggars is most disturbing. I have been there at all times of the day, hoping for some solitude or privacy, but each time come away exhausted and unsatisfied.

I never actually thought I would make it to Damascus, but my desire and emotional pull to pay my respects to the first, and greatest Muslim feminist of all times, Hazrat Bibi Zainab, landed me in Amman along with my British friend from London. She wanted to explore the Christian saints in Jordan and Syria and I, the Muslim ones. So off we went on our journey together, but with our different objectives.
We visited the Chapel of St. Paul in Damascus, and looked down the window where he was said to have been lowered in a basket to escape being caught after the crucifixion.
The Ummayad Mosque is overwhelming. John the Baptist (Hazrat Zakriya) is buried there and Salah ud Din Ayubi just outside. The head of Imam Hussain was placed there after being brought from Karbala, while Yazid sat and looked upon the survivors of Karbala. I could not believe that I was in this space where so much history had happened.

But my presence at Bibi Zainab's shrine is only for me to feel and keep locked in my heart, as one of the most moving experiences of my life. The greatness of this warrior from the house of the Prophet can only come to life when you stand before her and bow your head in recognition of her bravery and valour. I cried tears of joy at being in her presence, and tears of pain to recall what she and her family had to suffer at the hands of Yazid. That golden dome shining in the setting sun is an image imprinted on my mind.

We next went to the grand mosque at Allepo and stood in complete awe of the historical significance of where we were.

In Jordan, we did the Christian site of Mount Nebo, where Moses stood and saw the Promised Land. We saw the place where Christ was baptized by John the Baptist (Bethany Beyond Jordan) and across the small stream, we could look on Israel. I could not have thought at the time that I would actually visit Jerusalem and the birth place of Jesus and his burial place. We drove past the point where Prophet Elijah was lifted up to the Heavens. We dipped our feet in the Dead Sea and felt the salt in between our toes.

Trish and me at the UnmayadMosque, Damascus 2007

Paying homage to Hazrat Bibi Zainab
The first Muslim feminist in my opinion & my heroine of all times, Damascus 2007

Petra was a sight which makes me wonder at the brilliance and creativity of man. The majestic architecture, the superb craftsmanship of the carvings, the towering columns, the colour of the clay, reddish and brown, beautifully fused. Simply spectacular the first took my breath away.

I had harboured a burning desire to say my namaz (prayers) in the Mosque of Cordoba. I knew this could not happen but I still thought about it with passion and longing. How do I get to Spain?

But here I bow my head to the Almighty and His rewards.
Do you remember my Australian friend Bill when he visited us way back in the early 80s? He remembered you well when we talked about you off and on. He was the one who read the translation of your English poems with me in Honolulu to celebrate your birthday, when we were students together in the early eighties. It seems an age ago.

Anyway, somehow we got talking on our visit to the Jaipur Literature Festival and Spain came up in the discussion. He wanted to visit the Alhambra and I wanted to go to Cordoba. Hence, a plan was hatched. We met up in Madrid and started our train journey across Spain.
Seville, Granada, Cordoba, Barcelona. It was a magical trip.

But let me tell you about the mosque in Cordoba.
I guess there was some verse from Iqbal's poem of Masjid-e-Qartaba that has stayed with me. When I found myself before the Qibla in the mosque, I sat down and took off my shoes. Immediately I was accosted by a guard who told me to move on. I guess my head covering indicated I was a Muslim and there was to be no prayer here by law. I moved away, walked around a bit and came back, except this time I did not sit or kneel. I stood and said my nawafil (prayers) looking ahead as if I was a tourist, and tried to pour out

my gratitude to Allah for bringing me to this place of which I had dreamt of for so long and with such fervour.
Who says prayers are not answered? Who says dreams, if dreamt long enough, don't come true?

There have been countless other journeys to quench my thirst, and to provide answers to my restless soul.

Granada – enjoying a leisurely stroll in one of the palaces

Standing next to the Wailing Wall in Jerusalem, 2018

The Dome at first glance from Mount of Olives, March 24th, 2018 – The wind nearly blew us away

The shrines in Sindh of Shahbaz Qalander, Bhitshah, Sachal Sarmast; in Punjab of Pakpattan, Baba Fareed, in Kasur, Baba Bulley Shah, in Lahore Data Ganj Baksh, in Multan, Shah Rukne Alam; in Turkey, Konya, Mevlana Rumi and Shams Tabrez, in Istanbul, Ayub Ansari, in Ephesus, the house of Lady Mary; in Hebron, the tombs of Hazrat Ibrahim and his wife, along with Hazrat Ishaq; in Madina, my Prophet (PBUH) and many more. I pray they all heard my supplications and hopefully registered my presence as a devotee of their teachings and way of living.

Sinner that I am, I can only pray for forgiveness through the good offices of these great men of Allah to intervene on my behalf on the Day of Judgement. Ameen.

Standing beside the tomb of Hazrat Ibrahim, Hebron, 2018

This donkey was pretty tame in Petra, 2007

As Trish and I enter Petra, 2007

The gang outside Makli graveyard, 2017

دمشق مقام صلاح الدين الأيوبي
Damascus – Saladin's Mausoleum
Damas – Mausolée de Saladin
SYRIAN A.R.
60 SYRIAN A.R.
VITA NOVA
HOLLAND
Ali and Adeel Hashmi
156 - G - Model Town
LAHORE
PAKISTAN
پاکستان

Postcard

To
Ali and Adeel Hashmi
156- G, Model town, Lahore
From

Damascus (Saladin's Mausoleum)

Dear Ali and Adeel,
You must have read a lot in history about Damascus, the capital of the Umayyad Caliphs and also about Salah Uddin Ayubbi who was a very brave general and ruler of the Turks. That is why there are lots of historical buildings in this city, which are beautiful.
Congratulations on your success in the examination and lots of love,

Nana

پوسٹ کارڈ

To
Ali and Adeel Hashmi
156- G, Model town, Lahore
From

Damascus (Saladin's Mausoleum)

پیارے علی اور عدیل

تم نے تاریخ میں دمشق کا نام بہت پڑھا ہوگا جو اُمیہّ خلیفوں کا دارالخلافہ تھا۔ اور صلاح الدین ایوّبی کا نام بھی جو ترکوں کے بہت مشہور اور بہادر بادشاہ اور جرنیل تھے۔ اِس لئے اِس شہر میں بہت سی تاریخی عمارتیں ہیں جو بہت خوبصورت ہیں۔
تمھیں پاس ہونے کی مبارک باد اور بہت سا پیار

نانا

A road less travelled

I have heard so many times these comments, "You have wheels under your feet!"
"How come you have been staying put in Lahore for over two weeks?"
"How do you have so much energy to travel around all the time?"
"Don't you get tired of new beds, new hotel rooms, new foods?"
"It must be very tiring in and out of airports all the time!"
I keep wondering how many of these are asked out of genuine interest and how many because of...
To tell you the truth, I began to wonder if I actually inherited this "travel bug" from you.
You were never home long enough for us to get used to having you around. I took out your old passports and began a 'walk through' in your footsteps, stamp by stamp, visa by visa, year by year.

The passports were sort of falling apart with age and much handling.
But I was so curious and wanted to start mapping your travels. Some visa stamps were in Arabic, some in Chinese, some in French, some in Japanese. But most of them were, unsurprisingly, in Russian. I remember getting transported in time, looking at your passports, and finding myself waking up and finding you had left during the night. Where, would be my question. Mama would sort of mumble an answer. I wonder if she was even on board and knew where you were going, for how long, for what purpose. Because there were several times I heard you talk about how you went to a conference and met someone you knew there, who invited you to another place and off you went, and from there somewhere else and so on. And the journey sometimes ended up far away from where it had actually begun.

So I find myself documenting your travels from 1958 to 1984 from the only passports I could find in our archives in Faiz Ghar. There may possibly have been others which were misplaced or lost over the years. But I found it to be a most interesting exercise of walking in your footsteps.

So, I guess maybe this is why I would get restless after staying at home a few weeks and start itching to take off. That is why I sometimes accepted the oddest invitations to conferences and seminars and meetings where, I often had absolutely nothing to say or contribute. But I had accepted to be there, simply because I was getting restless at home, following the same old boring routine. Or it was a place or a country I had never been to and wanted to add to my list. For example, my visit to Doha was boring, so was Fiji, so was Macao. But I went for the experience, and to get away.

I have heard it said (or maybe read it somewhere) that creative people get restless and 'itchy' after staying put in a situation too long. Maybe that's what it was for you and possibly the same for me.
When I started a simple comparison of my travels to yours, I found a few similarities and also a few differences.

Let's look at your list and then mine.
The point of this exercise is not to do a one up on you or anything of the sort, but to focus on three of the most important trips which I made, and their effect on my spiritual and emotional well-being.

Let's begin with the first that I had mentioned earlier, Damascus and the reason for it.

Ever since Zainab, Adeel's daughter was born in 2004, I was intrigued by the fact that they had named her Zainab. I thought they would choose one of the trendy names going around at that time, but no, they chose Zainab. So I checked on the origin of the name and the story of Hazrat Bibi Zainab and promptly fell in love with this first Muslim feminist. Her story, after the Shahadat of her family and as she is being taken as a prisoner to Syria, and her address to the court of Yazid in which she flayed them for the treatment of her family and his lust for power, and how he (Yazid) would answer Allah for the mistreatment of the Prophet's grandson and the family made me cry every time I read it. I kept being pulled again and again to read the account of her being taken to court in chains, being made to look upon the head of her beloved father and other members of her family, and stand strong against the tyranny of the time. I could feel her pain, her agony, her heart stopping to beat every time she was forced to look around, her shame at the immodesty she was undergoing, her anger, her resolve to speak her mind no matter the consequences, her every muscle tense, her feet blistered with the long walk through the desert, her lips parched with thirst and yet her back upright, her eyes bright and focused and her words strong and direct.

Yes, I fell in love with this great woman and wanted to visit her shrine to pay homage to her memory, to her bravery, to her unflinching faith in Allah and His justice and to thank Him for giving us our Zainab, who, I hoped, would one day do justice to her name and the great woman she is named after. More on this in a while.

But how do I get to Damascus was the question.
As I now think back, I can see that the three most significant journeys I have made in my life have all been made after much thought, much longing, much planning and much spiritual contemplation.
So Damascus, and how it happened...

As they say, "When the stars are aligned, and the universe collaborates", the Syrian Ambassador at that time in Islamabad was an old, dear friend from many years earlier, as was our Ambassador in Jordan. Another precious friend in the UK decided she too wanted to go to both the countries along with me.

Attiya Mahmood, our Ambassador in Amman, was to be our host in Jordan and arranged our travel by taxi to Damascus.
Raid Ismat, the Syrian Ambassador in Islamabad (now deceased due to Covid-19), arranged my visa and gave me invaluable tips on what to see, where to eat, stay and what to wear in Damascus.
Trish Williams arrived from the UK a few hours after me in Amman as my companion on this trip, and off we went.

Our stay in Amman was most interesting and amazing. We had embassy support and our visit to Petra will always remain one the most magnificent and memorable highlights of all my travels, not to mention the donkey ride one has to undertake since it is a long haul in those ruins and, the day was sizzling!
But Hazrat Bibi Zainab's Mazaar visit, as I have expressed to you earlier, is my most precious memory. As we stepped out of the taxi, all covered in our black abayas and heads covered (which Trish was finding quite irritating but had to go along with it since it was a cultural and religious requirement) and walked across the courtyard to get closer to the shrine, tears started rolling down my cheeks. I could not believe that I was actually in the presence of this great icon, the granddaughter of my beloved Prophet (PBUH).). I stood before her with my head bowed in reverence and respect. I begged her forgiveness for all the agony, pain and sorrow she must have suffered watching her family members being massacred in front of her eyes. I prayed for her to rest in peace with all her loved ones in a place where they would be blessed and at rest. I beseeched Allah to give my own Zainab a happy and productive life, walking in the footsteps of this great woman after whom she was named.

As I closed my eyes and sat down in front of the mausoleum, I felt a calm flow through me. A cool breeze seemed to touch my cheek and dry my tears. I felt my heart lighten as if a great load had been lifted from my shoulders. Hazrat Bibi Zainab had accepted my homage and my presence.

I have to mention Trish here again to you. She watched me pass through this emotional catharsis from a distance. Being a Britisher, who loath to exhibit their feelings, I think she looked somewhat disconcerted by my very clear display of emotions and that too at a shrine. Although I had acquainted her with the position held by Hazrat Bibi Zainab in my heart, yet I felt that she could not have fully understood my response at the same time. I came and sat down next to her on the steps of the courtyard, exhausted by my melt down and the day's travel. I leant on her shoulder to rest my tired head and I felt the warmth of her affection flow through me. I looked up at her and she smiled, that gentle smile which said it all, "I don't understand but I do understand why you had to come here." I leant back again, this time closer, and closed my eyes. She put her hand across my shoulder and gave me a hug. I took a deep breath and stood up. My heart full of love, respect, friendship, peace. My work was done here.

I must have seen the image of Allama Iqbal praying at the Masjid e Qurtaba in Granada many a time. It was plastered all over our Urdu and Islamiat books. Over the years, a bug must have gotten into me for some reason, and stayed there biting me off and on. It was actually not Granada that intrigued me, but the desire to see Alhambra that would pop up here and there. Spain was just so far away, and how in God's earth would I get the visa and then how would I manage to book flights, hotels, tours, etc.

Iqbal at Cordoba Mosque in 1933

Alhamra – A dream come true

Granada – still gives me goose bumps

It was a never-ending story of impossibilities but it did not stop me from exploring and inquiring about the place. I wrote to a couple of friends who lived in Spain. They suggested tours. I got nervous and backed off. At some point the money I had saved for the trip dried up. Sometimes an assignment came up to prevent it from happening. Sometimes I just thought it was all a fuzzy thought in my head and I would grow out of it. But the bug kept chewing and nipping away, causing me to rethink yet again.
And then it happened.

I have already told you of my Australian friend Bill Lobban who was with me in Hawaii. He visited us in the eighties and met both of you. He and Mama struck up a friendship straight away. Gora to Gori! They shared the same jokes and nuances of the lingo. Anyway, I lost contact with him for many years and then somehow, thanks to the internet, we reconnected and became close again, sharing so much of our thoughts and lives across the seas. He lived in a small village somewhere up in the wilds of Australia, a recluse by choice. When I visited him on my way back from Fiji, I found out why. He was suffering from an incurable disease and wanted to spend his last years in peace and away from a world which he called, 'cruel and violent'. Anyway in our conversations over the next couple of years, we discovered our mutual passion to visit Spain. I was going to Munich for a conference. I told him I would join him in Madrid from there and we would go to the Alhambra and Granada together. A plan began to shape, just like that. Bill booked the train travel and the tours, and one hot evening in September 2015, I found myself outside the gates of Granada waiting to enter the Cathedral/Mosque of Qurtaba. We had taken the evening tour to save ourselves from the heat of the open skies, and as we entered the place I went into a complete daze. The glory of the inside of that grand building can only be experienced. It can only be felt through every pore of one's skin as one blends into the entire atmosphere. One walks around the arches which are apparently similar, and yet each is meticulously and individually designed. The colours of passionate red resonate as you find your way through the monument. Although there are dozens of visitors, there is a hush all around. People are talking in whispers. I found my way to 'the' mehrab (niche/decorative panel) which the guide was talking about and stood there in awe, thinking of all the great heroes and warriors of Islam who had prayed here centuries ago. I was in a state of ablution so I took off my shoes and sat down to say my nafal (prayers). A guard sprang up from nowhere and told me to stand up and put on my shoes. He stood there until I complied and walked away. I wandered around some more and came back, hopefully unobtrusively, but this time at a distance. I could see the mehrab. I did not take off my shoes this time. Nor did I kneel or bow down. I said my nafal (prayer) and asked for Allah's forgiveness and asked Him to accept my presence and my prayer. Bill found me later sitting outside looking somewhat sombre. "What is it? What happened?" I gave him my story. He laughed. "Mizu! You just don't give up do you?" I hadn't come all this way to "give up".

When the plan for Turkey started to get finalized, I told my young friend Maria who was organizing it, that I would only join on one condition. I wanted to visit Konya and pray at Rumi's mazaar. A long time ago I had heard that someone had asked you, "Faiz Sahib what is your religion?" and you had replied, "The same as Maulana Rumi's".

And "What is that?" asked the same person. You smiled, I am sure, your usual smug smile and said, "Same as mine". So I had to go and pay my respects to this great saint with whom you were so much in synch.

It was an almost eight hour drive. We reached Konya late night, totally exhausted, backs frozen in the bus ride, hungry and thirsty. Our hotel was a stone's throw away from our destination. The square was empty at this time of night. We walked around looking for food and at the same time soaking in the closeness of Rumi. The green dome sparkled in the moonlight. A cool breeze fluttered my hair as I walked around just trying to believe that I was actually there in the presence of this great man whom you held in such reverence. Our actual visit to the tomb was pretty much the same as for everybody else who came to pay their respects to this Sufi poet and teacher. My purpose was to pay respects on your behalf, because I never found out if you had actually been there. I could not find a Turkey stamp in your passport, so I guess this (hazri) or presence was due.

There was one place I know you did not visit, and it was a trip which has (since) changed my life entirely.

Your affinity with the Palestinians and Yasser Arafat is public knowledge. There are photographs and documents affirming your engagements in Beirut during your exile days. But my passion, or rather obsession, was to visit the Al Aqsa compound and pray there. As a Pakistani of course there was no way to do that, since our passport stamp says clearly that it is meant for "All countries of the world except Israel". However, when I got my British passport in my hand, the dream started moving on. Yet, it was replete with dangers. Areas occupied by Israeli troops, armed military guards, equipped with automatic weapons and threatening postures. These images appeared as hindrances in merely planning the visit.

Shatha, whom we had invited to the Faiz Festival in 2018, was a God-send from Ramallah. Over her last breakfast in Lahore, I mentioned a desire to visit Jerusalem. She came on board to arrange my trip, through Amman. It meant drive-through crossing over the Shah Hussain bridge. Saffina, my dare devil friend from London, agreed to be my companion and I found myself walking down the steps of old Jerusalem in March 2018 enroute to Aqsa! I was somewhat nervous, a bit trembly, breathing more rapidly than usual, holding tightly onto Saffina's hand, looking down so I did not slip or twist my foot on the cobbled streets, and then we found ourselves at the gate. Israeli military guards looked us up and down disinterestedly and we walked into the compound. Palestinian guards asked us if we were Muslims. We recited the Kalima and walked on. And then there was the Dome! And housed under it, the spot of ascension of our Prophet (PBUH). A look up the inner ceiling of the Dome is enough to soften even the hardest of hearts. The glory of the design; the stunning colours; the magnificence of its size is indeed staggering. I sank to the floor and bowed my head in reverence. In the centre is the rock from where he ascended. Under that rock is where he prayed. I could actually feel his presence and I feel his warmth, his acceptance, his blessings, I do wish you had been there to talk to me, to listen to me, to hear me describe these visits in person, because I feel no one can understand them better than you.

But I am telling you now and that is all that matters to me.

Praying inside the Dome in Jerusalem

With Shatha in Ramallah
She was our tour guide,
our support, our friend

What a magnificent museum in Doha, Qatar

Letter

002 /78
32 Church Crescent, London (N-10)
16 /4

Dear Mizu,

I received your letter on reaching here day before yesterday. It made me very happy.
This time we left home so suddenly that we could not even say proper goodbyes, but such were the circumstances. I am deeply concerned about you but we shall have to be patient for some days. Anyhow there is no need to worry because we are sure to meet sooner or later. Do not fret. There is nothing definite about our programme but shall probably have to go to Canada in two or three weeks. An invitation from there has been pending for quite some time. Then I also intend to do the Indian tour which had been postponed. There is a writers' meeting in Tashkent in early October and after that, whatever God proposes. I shall keep you informed. If you need any written content for your programme let me know the details. I have a lot of time on my hands these days.

Lots of love to Shoaib, Humair and the children. I shall write to the children myself too. We shall be seeing Dadi probably in a day or so.

With love,
Abbu

خط

002 /78
32 Church Crescent, London (N-10)
16 /4

پیاری میزو

پرسوں یہاں پہنچ کر تمہارا خط ملا، بہت خوشی ہوئی۔
ہم اس بار گھر سے واقعی ایسی افراتفری میں نکلے کہ آپ لوگوں کو ٹھیک سے خدا حافظ بھی نہ کر سکے، لیکن حالات ہی ایسے تھے۔ ظاہر ہے کہ آپ لوگوں کے لئے اپنا دل بھی ایسا ہی بیتاب ہے لیکن اب تو کچھ دن صبر ہی کرنا ہی پڑے گا۔ بہر حال تشویش کی کوئی بات نہیں، جلد یا دیر سے ملاقات ہو ہی جائے گی۔ تم لوگ پریشان نہ ہو۔ ابھی اپنا پروگرام بالکل پکا تو نہیں ہے لیکن غالباً دو تین ہفتے کے بعد کینیڈا جانا ہوگا جہاں کی دعوت دیر سے رکھی ہے۔ پھر ہندوستان کا دورہ جو ملتوی کر دیا تھا اسے پورا کرنے کا ارادہ ہے۔ اس کے بعد اکتوبر کے شروع میں تاشقند ایک ادیبوں کی میٹنگ ہے اور اس کے بعد جو خدا کو منظور ہوگا۔ تمہیں اطلاع دیتے رہیں گے۔ اگر تمہارے پروگرام کے لئے کچھ لکھنے وکھنے کی ضرورت ہو تو تفصیل بتا دو، آج کل ہمیں بہت فرصت ہے۔
شعیب، حمیر اور بچوں کو بہت سا پیار۔ بچوں کو ہم خود بھی لکھیں گے اور غالباً کل پرسوں دادی سے ملاقات ہوگی۔

پیار کے ساتھ

ابو

Actual Letter

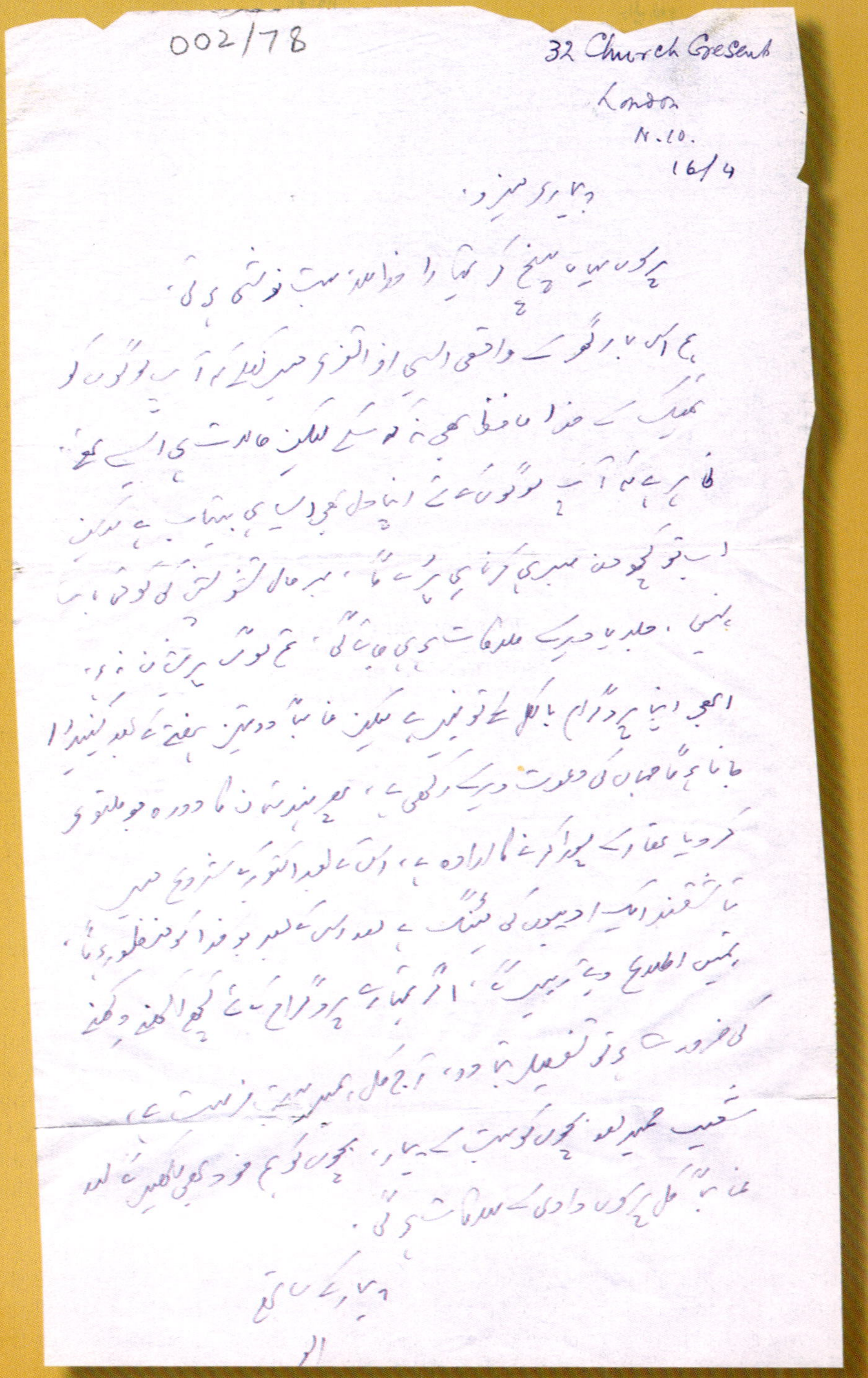

002/78

32 Church Crescent
London
N.10.
16/4

پیاری میرزو:

[illegible] پہنچ کر تمہارا خط ملا۔ بہت خوشی ہوئی۔

[illegible]

ابھی [illegible] پروگرام بالکل طے تو نہیں ہے لیکن غالباً دو تین ہفتے کے بعد کینیڈا جانا ہے [illegible] دعوت دے رکھی ہے۔ [illegible]

[illegible] اگر تمہارے پروگرام سے [illegible]

[illegible]

پیار کے ساتھ

ابو

Afghanistan... An Unforgettable visit!

I never got to ask you if you had ever visited Kabul, and if you did, what your impressions were.

If you had visited Afghanistan it would have been in saner times than when I went. I did hear from so many singers and other friends that they would just saunter into Kabul, watch Indian movies, shop until they dropped and come back through the Khyber Pass carrying loads of cloth and other stuff not available at home back then. Jashn-e-Kabul was another big attraction for our performers, as the Amir or ruler would invite them. Huge audiences greeted them. Big musical nights were organized and the performers were paid well too. But I don't recall your mentioning that you had visited. Anyhow, Urdu poets may not have been too popular, don't you think, because of the language barrier, whereas music is a universal language in itself, so can be heard and appreciated widely. I can just visualize our great singers such as Fareeda Khanum and Iqbal Bano, who did tell me they performed at Jashn-e-Kabul, singing Persian content, which would have found popularity amongst the listeners.

However, upon some more digging I found out that you and Mama did go to Kabul after the PDPA victory in 1978, with the overthrow of the royal family and establishment of the Democratic Republic of Afghanistan. You were invited by Afghan writers and Mama visited some women's organisations too. For the moment, that's all I have discovered. Maybe through this book, other information might be unearthed about that visit.
But let me tell you about mine.

Out of the blue, my British friend Trish Williams sends me an email asking if I would consider going to Kabul for the first ever Gender Training to be done through Internews, an international donor agency. The year is 2004/5. I am going through a rough time vis a vis PTV. I have been removed from my post as Director Programmes and side-lined as Director, PTV Academy, with no work and nothing substantial to occupy my time. There was a change of regime at the top, and as usual I was maligned as being on 'the other side'.

Me being me, with my usual impulsive inclination to take and make decisions on the spur of the moment, and then think them through later, agreed to go.
Besides, this was after the Taliban and Mujahideen era which I had followed over the years. The trauma and plight of the women of Afghanistan during both these political upheavals had me fascinated and traumatised both. The destruction of the Bamiyan statues despite international efforts to save them, made me weep inside. Seeing the blue burqas, forced on all women in Afghanistan, cut through my heart. When I actually tried one on in Kabul, apart from very nearly falling over with every step I took, I felt claustrophobic and restricted, as if I was being strangled. How those women lived in those times and with those 'moral' guardians, I will describe later. There were so many other horrific stories which I heard from the hotel staff and others during my visit.

I have always had a connection with Afghanistan as you well know, because of our family ties through my grandmothers and aunties and cousins, who are still a part of my life. Your father brought so many beautiful princesses and other royal family ladies with him as his wives when he was forced to flee the court.

Not many survived the heat and pauper-like conditions in this part of the world then, but the ones who did, were kind, beautiful, soft spoken and most loving towards me, and that was perhaps my pull to go to Kabul on that assignment.
I remember Adeel's reaction.
"How do you intend to go?" he asked.
"Via a UN aircraft," I replied, feeling important.
" And come back in a box?" he retorted.
That's when the reality hit me. What exactly was I getting myself into?
But I never back down so easily, right? You know that.

So I got on that UN plane from Islamabad. It was a small aircraft, more or less full of goras (foreigners). I wondered if they were feeling as nervous as I was.
The plane took off and we sort of skirted around Islamabad and then started our journey westwards. Since I was seated next to the window I had a clear glimpse of the scene below as the plane gained altitude. Traffic as usual, some animals grazing, roof tops, people, lots of green trees and some low hills covered with greenery.
And then suddenly, the landscape below changed.
What I could see now was barren land, no greenery, no trees.

I looked beyond, and saw dark, rocky mountains, grey, almost black, devoid of any life or colour, with jagged ends reaching towards the sky. It set the tone for what I would be seeing for the rest of my stay in Kabul. It was unwelcoming, unfriendly, unhappy, with a palpable negative energy.
A shudder passed through me. What am I doing here, I thought.

The plane took a dip and started losing height gradually, and then the dark mountains closed in. The bare earth rushed up to meet the wheels of the plane, and outside all I saw was a blank emptiness. A sense of cold set in as I saw ground staff, walking towards the plane, totally covered in woollies, faces covered and wearing thick boots. It was the middle of January, and certainly not the best time to be visiting a country recently recovering from an internal and external war, which had been on-going for decades.

As I walked out of the plane into a brilliant sunny morning, I saw a burnt tyre lying on the tarmac, and a few scorched birds sprawled around. Spots of oil, which had not been mopped up and turned soppy and black, dotted the tarmac.
I followed the line of disembarking passengers with a feeling of dread in the pit of my stomach. I had covered my head in the plane so was in the 'accepted' dress code. We had been briefed to bring with us only long sleeved and long shirts, no pants and several head coverings, etc.

Onay and I in D.C. in 2007

Walking through the immigration queue, I kept my eyes on the floor, picked up my one bag and walked out looking for my local host,
Onay Qasmi, who became my best friend, guide and my advisor in those tough four weeks was the most welcome face anyone could wish for. We still remain in contact after all these years and her beaming, warm, welcoming smile has stayed with me all this time. It was the same smile that greeted me on another sunny cold morning in Washington DC when we met up. She had moved there after marriage, a couple of years after we first met. This time we hugged and hugged trying to catch up for lost time.
So back to Kabul. The drive from the airport to the Inter-Continental Hotel, where I was to stay, was an eye opener.

There were only men on the streets, long beards, heads wrapped in thick turbans, black piercing eyes, thick chappals on dirty unkempt feet, shuffling as they walked. Shops were open as we drove past, but mostly of machinery, car spare parts, tyres, etc. Some fruit sellers stood along the streets, and I spied a policeman with hand cards to direct the traffic. Every single building along the way was barricaded with big cement blocks. We passed the UN compound, which looked like a fortress. I would be visiting it several times during my visit and would feel a sense of walking into enemy territory every time.
Well, I thought, so much for the excitement of visiting Kabul.

The Internews office, where I would be training young boys and girls, was situated in a house. It was nothing much to write home about, but comfortable. A cramped arrangement for the twenty odd participants who showed up. This was the first ever gender training which was being held in Kabul, and I of course had to be that very first trainer! These young men and women were actually sitting in a non-segregated environment for the first time in their lives! You can well imagine the 'fireworks' that would happen throughout the coming days.

The girls were making up for lost time, so wanted to speak loudly and all the time. The boys were not used to having competition from the opposite sex, or even to listening to their voices. And I was caught up in the crossfire of those energetic, vocal, intelligent young people who were just not going to let the other side dominate.
And then to top it all, Onay was herself a gender activist.

So when the debate became a bit more lively than it should be, she would throw in her lot with the girls. And the boys would get frustrated and complain to me for her siding with them. And I would just listen and watch.
Why did I only listen and watch?
Because by now the language would have invariably switched to Dari, and although I would catch a word here and there, the general tirade happening from both sides would go over my head. And I was that tennis match spectator, with my head swinging from left to right as the accusations were hurled back and forth.
Now, as I look back, it was a great learning experience, but at times frustrating, while I tried to keep peace and move on with my training plan.

I had to yell loudly at times to stop someone from shouting. I had to physically step in front of someone who was constantly screaming to tell the other party to shut up. I had to walk out too from a conflict situation a few times to bring matters under control.
I could see I was experiencing and facing an emotional explosion after decades of conservative thought, blocking of creativity, biases, prejudices. The girls were usually correct in confronting these conservative mind-sets. The boys did not like being challenged by them.

A few times I remember, when there was some quiet and they were all in a listening mode, I would remind them that this kind of behaviour was normal for both sides. They were actually witnessing a new national mind-set evolving. They were all a part of it and had a role to play in it. They were stakeholders and must take that responsibility seriously. I remember their innocence when I would begin to discuss this, and the look in their eyes was of wonder and disbelief. They did not have a clue about this new interpretation.

I formed a bond with many of them. They called me 'Ustaad' (teacher) which to me was so endearing. They were polite, respectful and gentle.

During break times, I would sit with the girls and ask about how the last few years had been for them. Horrific stories of Taliban atrocities were recounted for me. When I asked them to bring the blue burqa for me to try on, the landmark of the Taliban for all women, they found it funny. The next day when Parveen, a senior broadcaster did bring one, I tried it on, I kept tripping over the large skirt. I felt suffocated, restricted.

How these women survived six years of this torture is beyond me. I remember making fun of the white 'shuttle cock' burqas during my school days. Whenever we saw someone wearing one on the road, we would double up with laughter.

It was never a reality for me, and here I was, living it with these young girls.
Onay would often take me to her parents' home. They would feed me delicious dinners and let me be a guest in their warm and kind home. We would drive around town also, once in a while, and she would be my tourist guide. Her sister Seemin was the first, and at that time probably the only, female driver in Kabul. Sometimes, when dinner conversation got late, she would drive me back to my hotel, which was out of the city and up on a hill. We would be stopped several times at security checks and the guards would be surprised, and even annoyed, at seeing a young girl driving, and that too, late at night. The roads would be empty and I would be nervous about the drop-off every time. But not Seemin. Another sister Hossay, who is now herself a mother, was a young girl with pigtails then. She would also sit in the back seat with me as we drove along the almost empty and silent streets. I have to tell you that I was quite nervous throughout that journey, but not these sisters. Chattering away, they would swing along until we got to the hotel on the other side of town.

Sometimes after class, Onay and I would take the official car for a drive around the city. Onay was a great guide, but the stories she shared without batting an eyelid, were at times horrific and made my skin crawl. For example, once she took me to the stadium where boys were flying kites and playing football. We were of course covered from head to toe according to the SOPs, and as we walked around, Onay told me about the public floggings that had taken place right there, as well as some stoning of women and men for adultery. She described how the stadium was full of male spectators, who watched this gruesome ritual in silence. It made my blood curdle just thinking about it. Another time we drove past the roads where the Hazara community was lynched during Muharram by the war lord army. The skin had been torn off their backs, Onay told me, and I couldn't wait to get out of there.
I asked her why everyone in Kabul had a cell phone and there were no land lines. "Because the phone lines were torn up by the Mujahideen groups in an effort to destabilise the communications of the opposite side", she told me.

Houses everywhere still had bullet holes staring at us as we drove past. The buildings were crumbling from past warlords' confrontations. Paint was peeling off from almost every second house. Roads were non-existent, except the main artery running through the city. Side lanes were made of rough stones, and driving on them was jerky.

But what else do I remember...
That morning it was cold. Fresh snow was still lying on the ground. My joggers were quite ill-equipped to tackle any outdoor activity, but I wanted to visit Babar's grave. So Onay and I ventured out. The sun was brilliantly bright but the air was icy cold. The path to the grave was slippery and frozen. As we walked up the slope, I stopped to catch my breath and looked around. Beneath me lay the city of Kabul, covered in a blanket of white. From this height I could not see the open gutters, the beggar children, the blue clad burqa women treading carefully, avoiding any contact with males.

It was just a serene picturesque post card view of any city. Calm, with the sun rays catching the rooftops, some birds flying overhead and a horn blaring in the distance.

Babar's grave was situated under the open sky as he had wished it. Nondescript, with a white marble plaque with his name and dates of birth and death. It was surrounded by a rose garden, which due to winter was in some disarray. We were the only visitors that morning. Onay was on her cell phone, while I stood beside this great warrior who had changed the history of the sub-continent with his conquests. I wondered what exactly was I doing here in this very challenging country. I carried that sombre feeling with me throughout the day. That visit also led me to pay my respects to all the Mughal Empire kings, one by one, in India and in Lahore. Somehow, I connected with these great warriors. I read biographies and accounts of their reigns one by one. What grandeur, what might, what violence, what tyranny. It saddens me to think how man has not learnt from history or the past.

So back to my Kabul story. I had to find out more about what exactly had happened to women under Taliban rule. I asked discreet questions from my students, but they were all a bit too young to satisfy my thirst for more. Then Onay took me to see her grandmother. She was a podgy, matronly figure, sitting on a low stool. From her, I got descriptions of how the women of pre-Taliban times used to wear dresses and dance and move freely on the roads, she herself being one of them. I could not imagine this plump lady, now clad from head to toe, actually wearing a dress, but I took her word for it. Then came the Taliban, she said, and life changed. She described how they would burst into their homes to see who was not covered, and start hitting them with what she called 'cables', a thick wire. She stopped going out because no woman was allowed out without an escort. Once she did venture out to a neighbour's house and lifted her burqa just before she entered. She still carried the scar of the cable that slashed into her back from behind. A Talib had been following her, and gave her the punishment she 'deserved'. There were no wedding celebrations, no music, no singing, no dancing. If the girls did get together to celebrate, a guard was posted outside. As soon as a Talib was seen approaching, the celebration turned to wailing, as if a mourning situation was taking place. I found this whole description totally farcical. The old lady rocked with laughter as she described how she and the others would make fools out of the Talibs!

There are so many more memories of that visit, but this letter will get ever so long and might bore you.

Oh yes! I also visited a park, especially and strictly, only for women. It was a pretty place with girls roaming around freely, which was a pleasant sight. There were shops selling clothes, eatables, swings for kids, parkways to walk on. Sounds of laughter filled the air. The atmosphere was frivolous and the mood happy. The girls were generally very pretty. The burqas and chadors had been folded and put aside. It was 'time out' for these normal young and old females of Kabul: a few hours of living, a few hours of letting go, a few hours of being themselves. How much we take for granted, I thought, as I left. How much we need to be grateful for. How much we have, and some do not. Even today, after so many years, that vision of a young girl on a swing with her veil flying in the air and her giggles still makes me somewhat misty-eyed. Today, she is probably a mother of six and a grandmother of two.

Did you know that all the time when I was there, Kabul had electricity every other day? So when I suggested to Onay if I could come over to her house for a cup of tea, she would say "No Moneeza. Make it the day after. Tomorrow we don't have electricity". Can you believe that? In freezing temperatures, people were living without any hot water, heaters or lights except torches or battery lamps for three or four days a week.

Then there was the famous Chicken Street. I could not actually understand when somebody told me, "You have to visit Chicken Street while you are in Kabul". Why would I want to go visit a street selling chicken, I thought?

But no. Chicken Street is the most upmarket place in Kabul. Or at least it was back then. I am not sure about the name, or why it stuck in my head, but when I first drove down again with Seemin in the driving seat, I saw shop windows full of female dresses (not to my liking, but fashionable by Afghan standards), handbags and leather goods, very basic, but very neatly made and quite sturdy by the looks of them and cheap for my wallet. There were grocery shops selling foreign food stuff, for expats like myself. It became quite a weekly outing for me just to drive around there to pick up a bottle of Nescafe or cheese or Mayo for my sandwiches, or generally to see the city look alive. Women were walking around, with their heads covered, of course.

Men in their turbans and long beards, fiercely piercing eyes, rough hands, in Peshawari chappals stared at an odd 'gori' like myself driving along to pick up a snack or two for the next day. Street kids would surround the car and hang on, begging for 'baksheesh' (charity). They had beautiful green blue eyes, fair milky complexions, but dirty and smelly. They were certainly smart and clever with words and I was told never to even open the car window lest they pounce and grab my hand bag. I would watch their faces and be fascinated by their obviously Aryan ancestry as we drove past. If one of them caught my eye, he or she would run after the car, desperate for a dollar. Yes, they wanted dollars, not Afghani currency. They knew which side their bread was buttered!

Inter-Continental Hotel where I was staying, was being set up again after its destruction by the Taliban, who had mutilated the faces of the paintings on the walls and also dug up some of the floors. Such vandalism! The front desk manager was a Lahori from Samnabad, who, after my Faiz introduction, was especially kind to me, sending food up to my room, giving me extra time on the internet (which was my only connection with the world, and kept me sane in the long cold evenings when I returned to my hotel with absolutely no company and nothing to do). He also had prepared for me some of my favourite dishes like daal and sabzi, not meant for the Afghan palate, who are basically meat lovers. That hotel, surprisingly, had a beauty parlour hidden away in the basement somewhere, which I discovered by accident. The Thai massage was cheap and relaxing. I remember so many evenings of just disappearing there to get myself gently pummelled and stretched which ended up with a good night's sleep later. The General Manager, believe it or not, was a female from Iran. A charming person, she invited me for coffee once in a while and told me about the plans she had to make the place into a really fashionable and up market hotel. I wonder if she ever succeeded, but her hospitality was very welcome.

My mornings and afternoons were spent in training and the evenings were up for grabs. So, I would either drive around town with Onay, or go to her house for dinner or have a meal with the other goras around or spend it on the internet or watch soaps on TV in my room, sometimes wondering what I was doing with my life sitting in Kabul!
I am sure you probably asked that question of yourself in the many places you landed up in, except, my dear father, you had a wonderful pastime which I did not. You wrote poetry!

Babar's tomb in Kabul, 2005

Aa jao Africa

For ever I used to hear stories about Uncle Geoffery and Uncle Peter who went to South Africa 'to make their fortunes' and that got them cut off from Mama and Auntie Chris (Alys Faiz's sister who married M. D. Taseer and settled in Lahore). Since you and Uncle Taseer were 'darkies' as the term was used in those days for coloured people, there could be no communication with our side of the family. I did find out later that Mama, and presumably Auntie Chris, wrote letters to their brothers and mailed them to England. From there, their middle brother Teddy would send them on to Johannesburg. This whole process probably took a few months for replies to be received. When I met Uncle Peter in London many years later he told me about this long roundabout route of communicating with his sisters. He said Aly (what he called Mama for short) was far more regular than Chris. Since he was the youngest of the brood, I have a feeling he was closer to her than the other brothers.

Anyhow, so this thought of having a part of the family somewhere in Africa used to fascinate me, I remember.

I kept abreast of the apartheid movement and Mandela's struggle throughout my years in college. I followed that journey news item by news item, horrified at the violence and pain of the local people, sympathising with them as they struggled against the Afrikaans for their freedom, reading about Winnie Mandela leading protests, keeping up with Mandela's speeches to his people, and then being a witness of that heroic day when he walked out of prison and was later sworn in as the first black South African President. I saw the speech of his beamed live from that huge stadium, full of roaring crowds dancing and shouting with joy after suffering years and years of tyranny and injustice.

My South African maternal George cousins (L to R: Peter, Helen, Chris)

Johannesburg, South Africa 2018

Somehow, somewhere in my heart and mind was a strong pull towards this country. I wanted to feel the passion of these people first hand. I wanted to breathe the air of a country where freedom had been gotten after surmounting such challenges, I wanted to walk the streets of Soweto where Mandela had lived, I wanted to feel this movement which had moved you so much that you wrote your very powerful poem AA JAO AFRICA (Come Africa). Whenever I read it I felt energized. I felt alive. I felt full of hope and power. I felt invincible.

How exactly was I going to go there was a thought that never ever crossed my mind. Because it seemed so far away.

And then a training programme came up. It literally landed in my lap. I was asked to lead a team of young professionals, who were on their way to become media leaders, to Johannesburg. These were young brilliant people from India, Philippines, Ethiopia, Pakistan and Nigeria. We worked, laughed, interacted for three weeks. It was a memorable time where I felt the spirit of Mandela softly brush over me many a time as I walked around the shopping places and restaurants. We were cautioned all the time about not going out after dark and being careful with our valuables at all times. Nevertheless, there was never an incident to mar this fantastic period of learning, teaching, observing and enjoyment all rolled into one. We were working at the South African Broadcasting which was a stone's throw from our hotel. The weather was glorious. The morning breeze, when we walked to the training, was gentle and cool. The gravel beneath our feet was a yellowish colour. The flowers growing on the road side were pink and happy. It was a beautiful experience of connecting with Africa in a much broader sense than I could have ever imagined.

One of the trips scheduled was a day in Soweto. That morning I recall a feverish buzz of anticipation that could be felt within the group as we climbed into the minivan. A sense of excitement darted within me as we sped along the highway catching glimpses of life waking up in the smaller shanty towns as we drove past.
We were taken to Mandela's house in Soweto. The house is smallish with signs around to indicate his bedroom, his table, his dining table and the kitchen. I remember a hush came over us as we entered that 'sacred' area. I kept looking around for a sign. I have no idea what I was hoping for but it was as if I could feel a 'calling' from somewhere. Not a sound or a voice or a note, but just a tug, a pull, a breath. It's difficult to explain. I wonder if you ever felt something like that in a presence. Anyway we roamed around the small house and looked at the great man's belongings: his clothes, his books, his shoes, his eating plates, his spectacles, his pens. Perhaps I even smelt his aura floating around.

The next stop was the Church where the protestors were locked in and then shot. The bullet marks were still visible on the walls. As our guide talked away, I could almost hear the screams of the women and smell the fear of the children cooped up in that church waiting to die. The pandemonium that must have been happening, the panic, naked death staring them all in their faces. It all came back to me now even though it was more than twenty years ago. I just wanted to share this experience with you. I have never spoken about it to anyone before but I feel you will understand this connection with the violence and tyranny that happened with his people. The people of Mandela.
We stepped out into the bright sunlight and it was a relief to feel the sun rays caress our cheeks. It was a gift to feel alive that morning.

A visit to Desmond Tutu's house from the outside was the next port of call. Our guide told us about this great man and his bonding with 'Modiba' as Mandela is fondly called by his people.

The most impressionable memory of that day for me was our visit to the Hector Pierson museum. This place has been set up in memory of the march, when a young boy called Hector was shot by the apartheid forces and killed, as the demonstrators protested against bringing in Afrikaan as the language of instruction in schools. That shooting was the turning point of the protest movement, and after that there was no turning back for both parties. It finally resulted in South Africa's freedom and Mandela's Presidentship. It is a most impressive and beautiful building, which carries within it the history of the Apartheid movement, its heroes, its battles and its victories. Walking around it was such a poignant experience of understanding South Africa's struggle, its sacrifices and its triumph.

The drive back to our hotel was quiet and sombre. It was not only the tiredness from the journey, but the sense of oneness with this great struggle for freedom, which completely drained me. The winter dusk light over the buildings, as we approached our hotel, made one thing abundantly clear to me. I was born with this precious gift called freedom. How fortunate am I and how grateful I am to you and all the others who struggled and fought for this freedom. Myself and others of my generation have come to accept freedom as our birth right, but it was not always so. Immense pain and suffering was undergone to make it so. And I must never forget that.
Now what I have to tell will make you smile and your eyes twinkle. It is about connecting with the George side of my family. I didn't know the names of my maternal cousins but did have some idea about their whereabouts. How did I actually contact with my cousin Helen, my maternal 'Mamu' Uncle Geoffery's daughter, in Johannesburg is still a mystery to me. It was a random email I shot off and then forgot all about it. Mind you, this is after South Africa got its freedom. She responded and we started to correspond. Slowly but our friendship grew. She began to tell me more about the rest of her family, and I about mine, and so it continued until one fine day I got an invitation to attend a conference in Johannesburg.

As I walked out of my hotel that afternoon I can recall an odd knocking in my chest. There she was, my cousin Helen, with her husband Richard. We formally shook hands as she led me to the car. Conversation at dinner that evening in her house was easy and yet a bit stilted. There were some invisible barriers which would probably take years to come down. Photograph albums came out and I saw Mama as a young girl with her family, and that was quite a blast from the past as they say!

My next visit to South Africa, a couple of years later, included a visit to Cape Town where my other two cousins lived, Helen's siblings, Peter, the youngest, was jovial and cheeky. Just like Salman and just as good looking too. Chris, the eldest, was a doctor and quiet in demeanour. But we all became comfortable in each other's company, and I arrived back in Lahore with a heart full of memories.

A couple of years later to South Africa brought about a visit to Robbin Island. As the ferry bounced along the waves to the island, it was an eerie feeling of going back in time. I was desperate to see the cell where the great man had lived for years with only a small window to let in the sky. The cell is still etched in my memory as clear as day. I remember your cell in Sahiwal jail just as clearly, but that was bigger and somehow seemed more airy and more alive. This one was as small as can be, suffocating and tight. Twenty odd years is a long time to spend in such a place with no hope, no peace, no love. We walked around the quarries to see where he cut down rocks day after day, year after year. What resilience, what courage, what faith.

At the family dinner that night, my cousin Peter's daughter came up with a remark which has stayed with me since then. "Moneeza, what took you all so long to connect with us?"

Here, the phrase fits in perfectly. Better late than never. Just like this book.

Craft Bazaar in Johannesburg, South Africa 2018

And then there was Kashmir

Every time I would see that milestone just out of Murree pointing northward, saying "Srinagar .... miles", I would feel a tug somewhere, knowing that you were married there, and then hearing from Ammi (Humair's mother) about the beauty of Kashmir, I would feel an urge to visit. In Pre-Partition days, Kashmir was a summer haven to head for to avoid the heat of the plains. There was no load shedding then, I am sure, but there were also few other support systems to combat the soaring temperatures in those long summers.

I remember the 'charkao' (sprinkling of water) at night around the charpaiees (beds) with mosquito nets covering them, the pedestal fans being placed accurately enough, so that the last bed in the row got some air at least, the motia flowers (Jasmine) placed on the pillows to give off that heady perfume to lull one into exotic slumbers; the odd dog barking somewhere in the distance and then getting into a ridiculous argument with another one, this would go on and on as all such arguments do; the stars shining high. Yes, we could see the stars back then without telescopes and spectacles, and did they shine bright; some whispering at times and giggles too until being told off by a sleepy adult; the rising sun rays and chirping of the early birds bringing one back into the world of the living and another day began.

As I was saying before I got distracted.
Kashmir was the escape for all and sundry: the 'saabs' and 'memsaabs' (British officers and their wives), professors and their families, bureaucrats who followed the 'saabs' and many many more. Ammi would recount how Gulmarg was the most beautiful place on earth. She had actually at the time never been beyond Rawalpindi, and possibly an odd visit to Karachi, so her yardstick of comparison was limited, but she did plant the Gulmarg seed in my head.
I had to see it, but how?

The closest was that milestone outside Murree. Many years later, when the Indian Sarkar thought Cheemie and I (and several others) were non-threatening to their national security, we were given blanket visas on a yearly basis (no longer the case unfortunately). We explored much of India, attending conferences, meeting old friends, seeing new places, partying and whatever. It was on one of those trips that a thought suddenly hit me.

Why not Kashmir next time? I must say the thought was intimidating at first. Really? I thought. Should I? Could I? And then my adventurous spirit paid off. Why not? So I got cracking.
I found a tour online. Hugely disappointing I found out later but at the time at least I had a place to stay and it was affordable.

I told no one, literally no one of my plan. I crossed the border via Wagah, got to Delhi, stayed the night at a friend's, reported for an early flight to Srinagar the next morning and was on that plane.

The whole magnitude of this 'adventure' hit me when the pilot announced we were descending into Srinagar. I looked out of the window and saw a most breath-taking view of snow-capped mountains. I have seen many such views before on my visits across Europe, the USA, Canada, Russia and elsewhere. But these mountains had an allure, a mystique, a beckoning.

I have rarely felt so excited about any trip. There have been so many countries, so many trips, so many experiences, so many emotions.
But this was different, I could tell. This was going to be special and I could feel it. And different it was.

The moment I stepped out of the plane and stood on the stairs, I saw armed soldiers standing alert around the plane. Almost as if we were under siege or hostage and I had a tingling feeling of entering a not-so-welcoming space.
The next rude awakening was when, as a foreigner, I was pointed towards a separate reporting desk. A form had to be filled and handed over. My Pakistani passport of course aroused some (actually a great deal of) interest. My visa was examined minutely. Nothing wrong there. But I was not welcome here, I could feel that. I smiled my way out as I picked up my bag. My ride was late. I could feel that I was being examined over and over again. Finally he arrived and I was on my way.

What are my first impressions of Srinagar? Clean air. Blue skies. Women walking on the roads with heads covered. Young handsome men driving rickshaws. And the Indian army's presence. Army tanks and jeeps everywhere.
Concealed behind bushes. Soldiers holding weapons casually. Army cars racing around. It was definitely a city under occupation.
I did not know my driver enough to ask any questions, so keeping my counsel to myself, I just soaked in the fact that I was in Srinagar.

I forgot to tell you why I had decided on this adventure. I wanted to visit the guest house where you and Mama had been married. I had learnt it was now a girls' college. I had been in communication with the Principal, who was thrilled to invite me for a visit. I would take a few photographs, shed a few tears (I am stupidly sentimental on such occasions as you know) and be on my way. That was the plan. But as plans sometimes get twisted and turned, so did this one.

So where do I start?
My first impression of the famous Dal Lake.

Resting in a Shikara on Dal Lake, Srinagar 2016

The lake was dirty, muddy, its water smelly and the shores crowded with house boats, vendors yelling to get your attention. The house boat itself where I stayed was mouldy and damp, and had a house boy who was both sassy and rude at the same time. But I was stuck with it, so let's move on.

Basharat Peer and his lovely wife Ananya flew all the way from Delhi to 'show' me around Srinagar, and were waiting for me at the pier the next morning. We went off to visit the college which had once housed the guest house where Faiz and Alys 'took their vows', under the caring eye of Shaikh Abdullah, the Lion of Kashmir.

I was trying to keep my emotions under check as we drove into the compound, and were met by guards and a member of the college administration, and then escorted to the Principal's office who met me with great warmth and affection. After the usual greetings were over, I was escorted first to the library, which had been named the Faiz Library. Standing outside I became a bit teary, much to my own embarrassment and of all those around me. I walked around the place. There was Faiz Corner, which had a few of your books, mostly in Hindi. I promised to send them more. A promise to date I have not kept because of the logistics involved of getting the books 'out' of here and 'into' there. I came out of the library, which smelt terribly mouldy since the flood waters in the past year had swept onto the campus, affecting much of the furniture and equipment. Even after two years, the college was still awaiting financial aid from the Federal Government of India so they could start putting the place back on track. Meanwhile, the rot was settling in and walls were crumbling. It was a sorry sight I could tell. As I walked out of that library, an oldish lady walked up to me and introduced herself. She had met Mama on her one rare visit to the college, obviously many years ago, and Mama had shown her the actual room where she had got married and described the ceremony itself. Mama told her of her first glance when a 'tall man' came into the room and first spoke in Kashmiri and then in English, asking her approval for the nikah. Later on she found out who he was, Sheikh Abdullah himself. This lady took me to that actual room which was empty, as it was on the ground floor, and the flood waters had got to it. I stood in that open room and looked around trying to see Mama and maybe later, you. It was not quite what I had envisaged but it was a journey which I had to make to reconnect with a part of your life and hers, and where it all began. We had tea and I left among much handshakes and smiles.

Outside Faiz Library in Srinagar, 2016

The next day, Ananya accompanied me to Gulmarg. The road to Gulmarg, until we left Srinagar, was a nightmare. The traffic was horrendous, as was the noise and pollution, but once we hit the winding mountain road and smelt the pines and felt the cool air on our faces, it was glorious. That whole day (thanks to Ananya) was spent in sheer heaven.

Gulmerg – check the snowcapped mountains, Kashmir 2016

Gulmarg is beautiful. In fact that is too mild a word to describe all the natural splendour I saw around me. Being a week day, it was quiet. We had tea in a lovely hotel and looked at the rising snow-capped peaks. We walked in the garden and heard the singing of birds. We smelt the heady perfume of wild flowers. We heard the screeching of crows in the distance. It was idyllic and spell-binding and picture postcard beautiful. The day ended too soon and we were on our way back. That journey back for me was an eye opener, as Ananya explained to me the challenges of Kashmir, the trials of its people, the pain of the youth, and above all, an analysis of the bitterness between both countries. She put it so succinctly and simply. After so many years I was finally feeling light that Pakistan was not at the heart of all of Kashmir's problems. We may have aided and abetted the Kashmiris, but truly this was a festering wound of India, which had been mishandled, cruelly and insensitively dealt with and harshly treated.

I did the rounds of the city the next day, typical touristy stuff such as driving around visiting all the historical places. They were crowded but with local people. Foreigners were not around. Kashmir was still not quite the place to visit, I was told. There was just too much unrest at any given time.
Throughout that day I continued to see the obvious and visible Indian Army presence in my face.

The next day I decided to be adventurous and go shopping. I had seen some shops with beautiful embroidery, next to them was a dry fruit and honey shop. The rickshaw driver with whom I struck up a conversation was a young man. He was a college graduate with a widowed mother, driving a rickshaw to put food on his table. He was handsome, but with a sad face. It was an unsettling journey listening to this young man telling me his dreams, knowing he would not realize any of them, but dreaming them never the same. As I drove to the airport the next day, the driver, who was also the owner of the house boat I stayed in, told me how he had received a call every night, wanting to know where I had spent the day and if I had slept in the bed provided. Looking at my surprised face he said, "Madam, aap Pakistani ho" (Madam, you are Pakistani), as if that explanation sufficed. For him it did. For me it was unsettling to have been watched and monitored throughout my stay. It was the same feeling in Palestine, but more about that later.
The view from my window, as the flight lifted up, was again of snow-covered peaks. Ragged mountain ranges protecting the valley from whom? Us? Did I regret going to Kashmir? No, not for a moment. Had I expected it to be different? Yes, definitely.
October 30th, 1941 the day you got married must have been a cold day. Was there a log fire in your room? Did Mama have hot water to bathe? What did you both eat for breakfast the next morning? Did you take a walk as husband and wife while you were there?
Chacha Inayat (Faiz's younger brother) was also present at the nikah. Where did he stay? In the same guest house?

There was a mushaira the same night, Mama told me, so did your friends tease you, rag you on your wedding night?
Many questions still remain unanswered.
However, this trip to Kashmir did close one chapter and for me that was enough.

Faiz International Festival and Faiz Mela stories

After you left us and I had got over the pain of losing you and not having you around anymore, the idea of celebrating your birthday on a public level came up.

In 1985 we held the first Faiz Mela, or rather the first Faiz Memorial Lecture. In Alhamra. The speaker that first year was Professor Karar Hussain. As always the responsibility of the entire event, administration, arrangements and management gravitated to me. I am never quite sure if I seek out these daunting tasks, or if everyone thinks I am most suited to carry them out. Or is there 'a force' somewhere that simply chooses me and says, "Yes, her. Give it to her!" Anyway, I found myself booking the hall, arranging the sound, the stage paraphernalia, contacting the main speaker and finally, smilingly welcoming the guests as they walked in.

My loss in arranging and managing all these events, which when they started happening on a regular basis, is that I entirely miss out on actually enjoying what is going on. I am drawn in so many different directions, deflected by comments such as, "Madam, there is no water for the speaker." ("So go get it," is my answer, smiling, despite my angst), or "But do I have to sit in the sixth row?" (Yes, you do because you came late!) And so on and so forth. Usually, I am in shambles at the end of the event and happy just to go home and collapse.

"It was such a wonderful event. So well organized. How do you do it?" are comments I have been hearing now for years. I try to look humble or grateful, or even at times allow myself a tiny bit of pride. Though frankly, half way through the event, I am looking at my watch and thinking, "Gosh, how much longer is this gig going to go on?"

I can see you sitting somewhere in the front row, smoking and waiting for the event to finish. Anyway, so once that lecture happened in February 1985, it gradually became a yearly event to celebrate your birthday in Alhamra.
The next was a lecture by Ali Sardar Jafri.

It is such a pity that we never kept a record of those lectures. We somehow did not think of it then. Still, perhaps reeling from having lost you and with the onslaught of Martial Law added to the strain, day in and day out, I never got around to getting things more organized. I was under such scrutiny and suffering, such purgatory in PTV on an almost daily basis, that these matters had to take a back seat. Along with this, I had two young boys in school, their studies to monitor and the home front to manage. It all made my shoulders droop.

Another event that clearly stands out in my memory is the lecture given by Professor Abdus Salam at the Pearl Continental, Lahore in 1987.

How I got in touch with him is still a mystery to me, but again I found myself in the forefront organising the whole event. To be very honest, I did not comprehend the scale of the risk I was on taking at the time. I recall the security around the hall outside, I remember armed young men running with Dr. Salam's car as it entered the hotel vicinity. I remember his stocky figure as he came out of the car and greeted me. We walked into the hall, which was jam packed, with not even standing space. The young men who accompanied him placed themselves around the hall. I escorted him onto the stage and my job was done. As on numerous occasions, I waited for it to end, as by now I was feeling somewhat agitated and nervous.

I had the same anxious feeling in 2012, when I was invited by a young Indian professor to Chhattisgarh to attend an event celebrating your centennial. I asked a friend in Delhi, "How do I get to Chhattisgarh?" and she sounded horrified on the phone. "Why would you want to go there?' she asked. Later I find out that I am headed into the very heart of Naxalite land. No wonder she was concerned. Dr Arfa and myself landed there from Delhi one fine afternoon. We were driven to a large rest house and shown to our rooms. Later, the person who had invited us came to pay his respects. He was the grandson of Firaq Gorakhpuri but more visibly he was the head of the police force in that area. He was accompanied by armed guards who also came into our room and stood around watchfully. It was a slightly unnerving meeting. The next morning, after breakfast, when we entered the large hall packed to the brim with people who had come to honour you and your memory, I could not but help noticing armed guards again all around the large hall. I asked Dr Arfa what was going on and she told me that since this was Naxalite area, an attack could happen at any time! Certainly not a good omen to open a conference on peace, I thought. Then came the big gun again, and with him more armed guards who placed themselves close to the stage. I could not wait to get out of there fast enough. I flew out to Delhi the very next morning on the advice of friends and could not have been more relieved to see the back of Chhattisgarh!

All for the love of Faiz I thought, as the plane took off.
The Faiz Melas in your ancestral village are another experience altogether.
Arif Lohar, the folk singer star, was our biggest supporter and also the draw to bring in hordes of audiences. He never failed to engage the large mass of people in his funny and entertaining manner. For hours on end, the villagers lapped him up, singing with him, dancing with him and swarming the stage to be near him. It was quite a circus, which would give me anxiety attacks just trying to ensure his safety. Trying to control young village teenagers, who have never seen or been near a 'rock' star, is a daunting if not an impossible task. Their enthusiasm, exuberance, sheer abandonment of all norms of behaviour today seem amusing and even touching, but at the time, to me it was a nightmare and I would just pray that I would not have a major disaster on my hands. Somehow, it always worked out, and we would roll home the same evening, thoroughly exhausted after a challenging day.

Later, I decided to make this a PTV affair in that PTV would record the event and broadcast it. In addition, there would be security coverage as well as man power to manage the show. I had the most popular stage hosts to conduct the show. Mustansar Hussain Tarar and later Khalid Abbas Dar would keep the audiences in fits nonstop throughout the afternoon.

One performer, who I am so totally indebted to, is Inayat Hussain Bhatti. He was there two years running, singing his heart out. Driving his own car, not charging a dime for petrol, performance fee, musician's fee or anything else, that popular singer came to pay homage to you and your legacy. He was a great human being and a pleasant conversationalist, humble, selfless and calm in demeanour. I have the fondest of memories of sharing a cup of tea with him in my PTV office, discussing just about anything and everything.

Abida Parveen, the Sufi Queen and a lover of Faiz after her performance at the 3rd Faiz Festival in Lahore, 2017

Then there was the Big One in 1989, the year democracy returned to Pakistan. We got permission to hold the Faiz Mela, or Faiz Amn Mela as it had become, at the Railway Stadium in Lahore. I invited almost every performer I could think of: Allan Fakir, Khamiso Khan, Faiz Mohammad Baloch, Mastana brothers, Munir Sarhadi, Uncle Sargam and his team, Tufail Niazi and his sons, Arif Lohar, Surraiya Khanum, Tarannum Naz and more.

But the icing on the cake was Abida Parveen.
The crowd of thousands went ecstatic with each performer's presentation. Since it was open house for entry, the numbers kept growing as the day wore on. By sunset, it was an unbelievable mass of human beings, all in festival mode to express their relief after suffering years of repression under Martial Law, truly an awakening of the mass power of the people. I remember (and I have it on tape), Aunty Sheila Sandhu (comrade friend of Faiz), who had especially come from Delhi to witness the Mela and asked to sit on the stage throughout the proceedings, telling me, "Even in India I have never seen such a charged crowd". "You haven't suffered eleven years of Martial Law," I replied and she smiled. "And we didn't have Faiz either," she said.

There are so many stories related to the many Faiz Festivals and Melas. Some funny, some frustrating, some sad, some satisfying. Each festival teaches me a new lesson. Each festival brings a new challenge. Each festival unmasks new friends and foes. Each festival sets a higher benchmark. Each festival is a failure in some ways and a success in some. And after each festival I swear to myself: never again.

But then I am back the next year, looking for more punishment. I want to tell you two stories which are both hilarious and surprising at the same time!
We invited Naseeruddin Shah in 2015, as we had done before, to perform at the Festival. Sonam Kalra, the Gospel Sufi singer from Delhi, had also agreed to come.
The papers and documents for the visas were submitted well in time. I had met our Pakistan High Commissioner in Delhi, Mr Abdul Basit, who had been, as always, courteous and polite, assuring me of the utmost cooperation.
And the wait began.

We had a couple of phone calls and visits from some nameless gentlemen, and gave them the required details.
And the wait continued.

Cheemie went to see the Secretary of Interior in Islamabad and made the same polite request over a cup of tea and was again assured of all cooperation.
And the wait continued.

The dates started closing in.
The pressure from the public wanting to buy tickets started building up.
The phone calls from Naseer's Manager started coming at fairly regular intervals.
Sonam was politely asking whether she should book her seats from Delhi to Amritsar and if so on what flight, but I had no answer.
And the wait continued.

It was now early November. We were two weeks from show time. My WhatsApp messages to the High Commissioner were responded to with regularity and continuously the answer received was, "Madam we are waiting for the approval from Islamabad".

The Interior Ministry official who had so willingly answered my phone calls a couple of weeks ago suddenly stopped attending them.
We were a week from the festival. What was going on. We all kept wondering. A 'no' as an answer would have been less frustrating.
It was now four days to the festival. I was a total emotional wreck, trying to get answers from the Interior Ministry in Islamabad.
Around 8:00pm that night I received a call on my cell phone from an unknown number. I answered. "Madam. Main ------ bol raha hoon. Interior minister kay daftar say". I held my breath.

"Your visas have been refused. The Minister says that our artistes are not being provided visas, so why should we give visas to the Indian artistes. Also, he says the Ministry was not given enough time to process the visas". That was a complete fabrication! We had given them more than the time required to process the documents. What do they take me for, a novice? I know the games you guys play and I know them well. I had planned it down to the minutest detail of making sure there was no such silly objection. So don't give me that kind of excuse. Just pull that damn rope and let me hang, is what I felt like saying, but of course I didn't say any of it. I just took a deep breath as there really wasn't much to say after that remark.

"Shukria" (Thank you), I said and hung up.
I don't think I shed any tears, but the feeling of utmost sadness and a sense of failure hit me in the gut. I took a deep breath and called Cheemie.
"The visas have been refused." "What?"
"Yeah," I said. "Let me now tell the Indians."

I sent Sonam a WhatsApp message with deep regret in my heart and with an apology. She answered back almost immediately, with words of disappointment and comfort. I did not have the heart to call Naseer's manager just then. I decided to say my Isha prayers and sat down to do so.
The cell phone rang again. It was the same number as before. What does he want now, I thought.
"Hello. Madam main ------bol raha hoon Interior Minister kay daftar say." (I am ---- from the Minister's office.)
As if I could forget.
"Ji?" (Yes?)
"Madam Minister sahib keh rahay hain kay Madam nay aaj tak kuch request nahin ki tau yeh request main unki agree kar raha hoon aur aap kay saray visay approve ho gayay hain." (Madam, the Minister says that you haven't asked for any favour ever before that is why he is agreeing to this request of yours. All your visa applications have been approved.)

Imagine my reaction!
"Please hamara shukria Minisiter sahib ko pohncha dain." (Please, convey our gratitude to the Minister.)
"Madam aap ka koee fax number hai tau main aap ko approval fax kar doon?" (Madam, if you have any fax number, I can fax you all the approvals right away.) says he.
Fax number? In this day and age? Was he serious?
"Fax number tau nahin hai". (There is no fax number.) I could barely put my rapidly distracted and distorted brain back on track.
"Acha main aap ko WhatsApp kar daita hoon."(Ok! I can send you via WhatsApp.)
My WhatsApp started to tingle and tingle and tingle.
The approval letter, with all the names of our guests, started rolling off my screen.
I called Cheemie with the good news. She went ballistic.
"Why can't they make up their minds once and for all?"

I sent another message to Sonam with the good news on WhatsApp. This time she called back to make sure she has heard it right, laughing and humming.
I forwarded the same WhatsApp message to the High Commissioner, although it was by now almost 10 p.m. in Delhi. He promised to set his Visa section in full gear the next morning.

But wait, the matter was not over yet. The next day this person in the High Commission called and his name was Faiz!
He said that he would be scrutinizing the documents that had been sitting with him for a month, and then now, suddenly all hell breaks loose because I was on the line from Lahore and he was sitting in Delhi. The clock was ticking. I was chewing my nails, counting the hours. I am calling him every three or four hours. "Faiz Sahib. Ki banaya?" (Faiz Sahib, what's the progress?)
"Madam aap ka hi kaam kar raha hoon. Kuch forms ghalat bharay hain. Woh bhi theek karnay hain. Hum kal raat 10 bajay tak bhaitay rahay thay." (Madam, we are busy working on your task. A few forms were filled in incorrectly, we have to fill those correctly as well. We have been working till 10 p.m. last night.) I kept telling myself, back off lady, don't annoy him. Let him work at his own speed even if it is slower than you want it to be.

And the visas were done. Now began the long process of getting people to go collect their passports. Entering the Pak High Commission in Delhi for Indians is just as difficult as entering the Indian one in Islamabad is for Pakistanis. Countless checks, invisible eyes watching, long waits. Finally on my last call to Faiz he tells me, "Madam aap ka kaam khatam ho gaya hai. Next time please thora time ziada dain." (Madam, we are done with your task. Please ensure availability of more time in future.) No point telling him the gruelling story of how the visas were granted!

After the thank yous were over, you would think it's all done. Right? No way. There is still one more episode to be written.
So Naseeruddin Shah and his team's passports had to be collected and delivered to them inside Delhi airport on the morning of their departure for Amritsar, from where they would cross over the border on foot. How was I to ensure the passports would be delivered? I tried several friends, asked around, but no one would be allowed into Delhi airport without a ticket to a flight, and Naseer could not come out of the airport either.
I kept getting calls from Naseer's manager, Jairaj.

"Moneeza madam. Hamaray passport?" (Ms Moneeza, our passports?) I kept telling him "I'm working on it. Aap bus flight pakar lain. Baqi main dekh loon gi." (You just catch your flight, I will take care of the rest.)

Sonam Kalra who was coming to the Festival a couple of days later understood my predicament. She sent her assistant to collect Naseer's team's passports from the High Commission. She bought a ticket for her driver (which we paid for of course) to be on the same flight as Naseer from Delhi to Amritsar and back the same afternoon! She handed her driver the passports with instructions. Naseer caught the connecting flight from Delhi at 8:00am. As soon as the flight took off, Sonam's driver left his seat and walked to the business class section of the plane, handed over the packet containing the passports to Naseer, who received them with thanks. The driver had his moment of meeting a star he had admired for long and returned to his seat. The plane landed in Amritsar, and Naseer's team had their passports duly stamped with the visas in hand. A van awaited their arrival and raced them to the Wagah border. They crossed over to the Pakistan side where I was waiting with bouquets and tears in my eyes! We hugged. Naseer said, "Exactly how did you manage this?" He performed to packed ecstatic houses for three days, two shows a day.
Your magic name (Faiz) had swung into action again!
The second thriller happened in 2018.

We had invited Shabana Azmi and Javed Akhtar to be with us that year. Again it was a tight squeeze to get their passports sorted out, and sent to the High Commission in time for visa stamping. The commendable visa staff at the High Commission was constantly coordinating with me. I had to again get the personal assistant of a friend collect the passports from Delhi airport to where they had been graciously hand-carried from Mumbai by the pilot! He raced to the High Commission, where the staff was on standby. The visas were stamped in two hours. With one part of the mission completed, now the question was where to deliver them. Javed had instructed that the passports be handed to him in his hotel room in Delhi, (where he had arrived the same morning from Mumbai) between 7:00 and 7:30pm that evening.

Shabana Azmi crossing Wagah Border for the 4th Faiz Festival, 2018

Javed Akhtar says good-bye to Lahore after the 4th Faiz Festival, 2018

Shabana was to reach Delhi from Mumbai the next morning. They were booked on the morning flight to Amritsar the next day. So far so good, until there was a catch, as usual. The flight from Delhi was to depart at 12:30pm, reach Amritsar at 1:30 p.m. and the border closed at 3 p.m. So, it would be a super dash to make it in time to cross over.

In comes Arvinder Chamak, a friend in Amritsar who is charged with the responsibility to get them to the border in time!
He did.

Not only that, he arranged a car to drive them to the no man's land with full protocol (instead of the usual bus ride), and there I was waiting with flowers again. This time there were no tears. The granting of the visas by Pakistan had been the easy part. It was the timing that was crucial and that too had miraculously worked.

And Lahoris, true to their tradition of welcome, gave both the stars a standing ovation in a packed to capacity hall that evening which gave me, once again, a sense of relief and achievement when I put my weary body to bed that night.
There are times I wonder how I get into and out of these situations.

Do I look for such nerve biting happenings? Not really. They find me and then test me and push me to limits of my endurance. That is something I had learnt from Mama but not in a formal sit down lesson. Throughout my life I had watched her cycling in the heat to get to office; scrimping and saving to fulfil our needs; taking rickety and hot dusty train journeys to spend a few hours with you somewhere across the country in jail; wash her own and our clothes by hand; pay bills beyond her earnings somehow, without asking anyone for money (or even if she did, she never let on). Her British sense of decorum and dignity prevented her from breaking down or showing any weakness. That was my role model. That is what I imbibed as I was growing up, plus, of course, the George genes, as Puppi (Shoaib) used to laughingly point out to Humair.

Faiz Peace Festival, London, 2016

The earlier Faiz Aman Melas, as they were called, used to be held in the Open Air Theatre. This was during the Zia era. They became a symbol of defiance, and the numbers grew with each passing year. And who would have to control those milling crowds of enthusiastic left workers, the students from banned student unions, and the general public, who wanted to exhibit their love for Faiz by simply being rowdy and disruptive? You guessed it. Yours truly. Those few hours tested my strength to the limit, both physically and emotionally. There were intelligence or CID agents, or whatever the government spies were called at the time, watching and reporting.

I was an employee of PTV at the time, which is one of the essential services, which meant that all of these anti-Zia slogans were being entered in my personal file somewhere. The crowds would surge to the stage and at times be physically removed by me, sometimes by cajoling, sometimes by threats, sometimes by begging, sometimes by acting tough, sometimes by bullying. But each time a general order would be maintained successfully until the event ended. It of course took its toll on me, but I learnt to get tougher every year and more management savvy, which helped in the later PTV years of my career, when I was dealing with the ruffians of the Union, who were just as destructive and disruptive.

But one Mela to be remembered with pride was the one we organized in the Railway Stadium, as I have earlier mentioned. The Pakistan People's Party had just come into power after eleven years of Martial Law, and I expected a bigger crowd that year. I was not wrong. I wanted a bigger venue to hold the crowds and I was not wrong. I wanted to show that Faiz's vision was still alive, and I was not wrong.

I negotiated with PTV to cover the Mela and broadcast it across the country. This was probably the best decision anyone could have taken at the time. It took the Mela out of Lahore to the country and worldwide.
I have it all preserved on a VHS tape, but of course in time these technological systems get rusty and die a natural death. I doubt if PTV has even preserved this iconic festival, but the memories live on.
As does Faiz…

Iqbal Bano singing your famous "Hum dekhain gay" in Alhamra Hall 1 is another event etched in the hearts and minds of the hundreds of Faiz lovers who gathered that February to wish you a happy birthday. The hall over-flowed so I had the doors opened up. People sat on the stairs outside listening. I bet the 'silent observers' were all over the place, but there was no clash or confrontation.
This was the first time she brought this poem to the public. And what a thundering ovation she got.
What spirit, what enthusiasm, what joy, what exhilaration!
And since then 'Hum dekhain gay' has become the anthem for all protests, all resistance movements, all human rights demonstrations, political discourses and even drawing room conversations. Today, the farmers in India are singing the Punjabi translation.
When the Gulf War began, no one was in the mood for Faiz Mela celebrations, but the show had to go on.

So it was decided to hold a qawwali night instead.
Nusrat Fateh Ali Khan agreed to perform, and for the first and only time, added a Faiz poem to his repertoire. I still have the tape. We never released it. It was again a sober and magical evening. I recall I negotiated Rs. 12,000 payment for this iconic performance. He sat in my room in PTV, and over a cup of tea we talked about how the evening would go. Rahat Fateh Ali Khan, then a young boy, accompanied him.

Corona Day
9th April, 2020

I cannot remember which day of lockdown it is today. This is getting beyond ridiculous, and also at times beyond comprehension and patience. But has to be endured.
Guess what? We met last night…in my dream.
It was just like any other night, except it was the middle of Shaban and Shab-e-Barat.
I said my Isha prayers and prayed simply for the health of all my family and friends and this country and the world. What else can you pray for in these trying times?

Anyway, I then watched two episodes of my nightly soap and went to bed.
What I then recall vividly is that I was in a book launch of someone I did not actually know too closely. There were people around and we were walking around Islamabad Club. Not in the grounds or anything but just sort of meandering around talking, the usual meaningless conversation. In my dream, I cannot recognize any person as such.
So we walk around.

There are other people also, just drifting about as they do in clubs.
There are flowers around too, and then suddenly, I look to the left, and there you are.
You are walking to our group with that usual smile on your face and a look of "Am glad I made it". You are wearing your usual tweed type attire with a muffler or scarf around your neck.
And my first reaction is a smile which breaks on to my face and I exclaim, "There he is!" as if I was waiting for you to show up.

Yes, that's what I felt. Almost relief that you had showed up.
You walk to the group and there are greetings all around.
And then you walk towards the right as if you are going to call a waiter or someone. And I hear a voice saying, "Can I help?" And you return to the group smiling but don't say a word.

And I wake up with the sound of the Fajr azaan (Call for Morning Prayer) and say my prayers.
I say two nawafil for you and Mama, as I do with every Fajr prayer, and then lie down for my last part of the night's snooze.

This is really sometimes the best way for me to immerse into the world of the unknown. Often I do not actually go under, but float around in my REM stage and even that is a pleasing feeling of in between two consciousness states.
The dawn sneaks in through my open curtains and the day begins to make itself known. The birds wake up chittering and chattering about this and that. A light breeze brushes my face, making me thankful to be alive. The sounds of a household waking up downstairs become more pronounced.

These days there are no horns or motor bikes roaring on the roads.
Just the odd gate being slammed shut. I take a deep breath and decide to get out of bed.

It was a chance meeting, but after too long. I miss you Abu. Can you lift that curtain once in a while and come back? Just a brief reassurance that you are there watching my back and reassure me that these dark days too shall pass and the birds will chirp again. Grandkids will be squabbling and cribbing about homework and exams' preparations. Maids will be more exasperating and demanding. I will get short tempered and anxious about preparations for the next Faiz Festival, and where the money for it will come from. Can we talk again soon, please?

The actual only posed photograph of both of us which I cherish

Letter

004 / 80
Beirut. London
5 March

Dear Mizu,

I have not received a letter from you for quite some days and I am sorry that I could not write either because of commitments, but Cheemi's letters keep us posted about your welfare.

It has been extremely cold the last two or three weeks and also been raining constantly, which, people say is a first. Now, the weather has opened up, reminding me of Lahore's balmy 'pink' winters. My programme is something like this… breakfast around eight or nine and then from the room in the house to the room in the office across the road. Then lunch at two or three and a short nap after that. Your Ammee puts in two or three hours in the city's streets and alleys. I just take a breather for fifteen minutes at the most, very rarely venturing out for a movie with your Ammee that is, if I really make an effort for it. Evenings I watch the most disgusting television that there ever was. Occasionally there is a boring party to be attended. The rest of the time I read something and miss you all or listen to the sound of flying bullets. But these sounds are quite distanced from us and our area is totally peaceful because no leader lives here. Otherwise it is very comfortable here and nothing bothers us.

Lots of love,
Abbu

خط

004 / 80
Beirut. London
5 March

پیاری میزو

بہت دنوں سے تمہارا کوئی خط نہیں آیا اور مجھے افسوس ہے کہ مصروفیت کے باعث ہم بھی نہ لکھ سکے لیکن چھیمی کے خطوط سے آپ لوگوں کی خیریت معلوم ہوتی رہی۔

یہاں پر دو تین ہفتے بہت کڑاکے کی سردی پڑی اور بارش بھی مسلسل ہوتی رہی جو لوگ کہتے ہیں پہلے کبھی نہیں ہوا تھا۔ اب موسم کھل گیا ہے اور لاہور کے گلابی جاڑوں کی یاد آتی ہے۔ اپنا پروگرام یہ رہتا ہے کہ صبح آٹھ نو بجے ناشتہ کرتے ہیں، پھر گھر کے کمرے سے اٹھ کر سامنے والے دفتر کے کمرے میں جا بیٹھتے ہیں۔ دو تین بجے کھانا کھایا، ایک آدھ گھنٹہ سوئے۔ دن میں تمہاری امی دو تین گھنٹے شہر کے گلی کوچوں کا لگاتی ہیں۔ ہم زیادہ سے زیادہ پندرہ بیس منٹ ہوا کھاتے ہیں اور بہت ہمت کی تو کسی دن امی کے ساتھ فلم دیکھ آتے ہیں۔ شام کو عام طور سے نہایت گھٹیا TV دیکھتے ہیں۔ کبھی کبھار کسی بور پارٹی میں جانا ہوتا ہے۔ باقی وقت کچھ پڑھتے ہیں اور تم لوگوں کو یاد کرتے ہیں یا گولیاں چلنے کی آوازیں سنتے ہیں لیکن یہ آوازیں دور سے آتی ہیں۔ ہمارے محلے میں بالکل امن ہے اس لئے کہ یہاں کوئی لیڈر نہیں رہتا۔ ویسے یہاں آرام بہت ہے اور کسی چیز کی تکلیف نہیں۔

بہت سا پیار

ابو

In Palestine

Why Palestine? It was the wish of praying at Al Aqsa that has haunted me for so many years. I would read about what was happening in the compound, the protests, the lathi charges, the tear gassing, the closing of the premises for the Palestinians and all of that. But I wanted to see it for myself. Plus there was, and is still, a romance with Palestine. For me that is. I have met so many people across the world, at conferences and seminars, and heard their stories of pain, separation, displacement, seeking a life out of their own country, destitute at times, desperate. How do you go on living a wretched life and still hope? How do you go on residing temporarily in countries without roots? How do you go on praying without any sign of an answer? Simply put, how do you go on living.

Saffina, my travel companion and saviour on this trip who joined me from London, made a random comment which shook me to the core. As we walked across the Israeli check post on the way back to Amman via the Hussain bridge crossing she said, "Well that was the best gift your mum could have given you." She meant the red British passport and she was right. I, in that moment, completely and utterly felt a lightness of being as I said thank you to Mama, and all those years of feeling neglected rolled away. In that moment, we connected.

So Palestine 'just' happened. A chance remark at an impromptu breakfast meeting with an acquaintance who offered to host me in Palestine and the seed was sown!

Climbing up the steps on the Mount of Temptation, Jericho, 2018

Three months later, Saffina and I were loading our bags into a taxi in Amman and driving to Hussain bridge to cross into Israel/Palestine.

We had our moments of anxiety when the immigration officer, who had the most beautiful eyes I remember, asked us twice about our 'connections' with Pakistan and we answered twice, as dead pan as possible, that we had family there (true), that we did not intend to work in Jerusalem (true), that we were tourists (true), and we would return in a week (true). Maybe it was my grey hair that convinced her or Saffina's very innocent answers, but we got that piece of paper and walked out into the bright sunshine into Israel/Palestine, relieved and thirsty.

You never went to Jerusalem did you? You couldn't, I guess, as your green book would not permit you to enter. So I did experience a heady feeling that I was going somewhere you had not been. No easy feat, judging by your wanderings all over the world!
That first look of the Dome from the Mount of Olives took my breath away. It was a cold and windy morning, but the view was amazing from up there.

Inside, when we walked into the compound photo, the feeling became more intense as we were entering the holiest of sites. The memory of standing in a place where hundreds of years of history is buried, still sends shivers down my spine. Entering the mosque and looking up at the magnificently decorated and ornate ceiling was astounding. Walking towards the Dome inside and laying eyes on the place from where the Miraj took place cannot be described. Saying nafals and namaz within those walls is probably the dream of every spiritually alive Muslim and I had achieved it.

I wish I could have told you face to face about that feeling of cleansing, of peace, of experiencing a closeness to the Prophet (PBUH), and just feeling calm at actually being in a place I could call home. But I guess writing you this letter is the next best thing.

Standing at the great man's mausoleum in Ramallah, 2018

The rest of the trip was wonderfully satisfying. The Church Sepulchre, where Christ was buried and from where his body was resurrected; the Wailing Wall; Bethlehem where Christ was born, and Nazareth where he grew up; Hebron where Abraham and Ishaaq are buried along with their wives and Jericho, where Satan tempted Christ to denounce God were amazing experiences.

But perhaps the most moving for me was Ramallah, when I stood at the grave of Yasser Arafat. It was not just an emotional moment, but I saw you both together in Beirut – laughing, talking, sharing, discussing. Buddies as you were. And suddenly I understood why I had to visit this country under occupation, taking unnecessary risks along the way, feeling nervous throughout those five days, looking over my shoulder, at times, in case someone was shadowing us, not asking too many questions or drawing attention to ourselves, trying to blend in with the locals (though not too successfully), just pretending to be normal tourists. I had come to connect with you and through you, to Abu Ammar. I had come to connect with the Palestinian cause, its people, its struggle, its pain and its hope.

Both your smiles say it all, Beirut 1979

When I saw the walls built in Bethlehem, I wondered how the people of that city could live with that monstrosity encroaching on their freedom.
When I saw the streets in Hebron covered with mesh, to protect the people walking in the streets from the filth and slime the settlers threw at them from above, I wondered at their patience.

I was aghast when I saw the barbed wires encircling the olive gardens and taking them over forcefully from their rightful owners; when I saw the Mosque of Ibrahim divided by soldiers guarding its entrance asking for passports before entry; when I saw armed militia outside the Al Aqsa compound appraising everyone who was walking in; when I had to walk down a dark corridor to cross from Bethlehem to Jerusalem and show my British passport, while my host (who lives in Bethlehem) could not accompany us because she carried a Palestinian travel card, and when I walked the streets of Hebron, and saw, behind veiled windows sharp eyes and weapons pointed at all passersby.
I became a part of their struggle. I identified with their tears. I felt their hopelessness. I became Palestine.

And now I understood your poem.

Letter

004 /81
Beirut, Lebanon
March 3

Dear Mizu,

I received your card here a couple of days ago and yesterday, a letter. Your Jalsa was a success and that makes me happy. The news about the Lahore Jalsa was printed in the Jang. You read it for yourself. There were two huge Jalsas in Moscow. Lots of people came to attend. Lots of laudatory speeches written on very expensive paper were read out. I have brought them back here. My old friends, the ambassadors of India, Bangladesh and Palestine as well as our ambassador Iftikhar Ali were also there. Evtushenko and Vosnozenski the two Russian greats who are never seen together, also came and read out Russian translations of my poems.

I have also received a medal from the Friendship Society but I got the greatest pleasure from Yasser Arafat's message which is attached to it. Get it translated from somebody who is good at Arabic. Many organizations were insisting for a February 13th Jalsa in England but they are all constantly in disagreement with each other so I did not commit to anybody and quietly went off to Birmingham. There I had a friends' meet up at a mate, Badr Saheb's house. Saleem Shahid, Zia Mohyuddin and his wife Naheed, Naheed Niazi and some other friends got together and enacted quite a few folk traditions. The girls put up an "Arthi". The hosts gave away my weight in meat as a special gesture to keep evil at bay! But sorry to say that the very next day my old friend Afzal passed away suddenly and so the next few days were spent in mourning.

Your Ammee is still with Salma so the loneliness is making me feel wretched. I also plan to go there tomorrow and will return next week with her.

Dr. Ijaz called in London but I did not get to talk to him since I was out of the house. Give my love to the couple and regards to his father if he is there.

You write about missing the children and your house but that is something that has to be suffered by anybody away from home. Your period of separation is not all that lengthy and God willing, the same for me. You have asked about the ticket money. Well if the University agrees then well and good, otherwise a one-way fare, however much it may be, is on me. When the time comes then write to me instead of to your mother.

Lots of love,
Abbu

خط

004 /81
Beirut, Lebanon
March 3

پیاری میزو

دو چار دن پہلے یہاں پہنچ کر تمہارا کارڈ اور کل تمہارا خط ملا۔ تمہارا جلسہ کامیاب رہا جس کی خوشی ہے۔ لاہور کے جلسے کی روداد جنگ اخبار میں چھپی ہے تم خود پڑھ لو، ماسکو میں دو بھاری جلسے ہوئے، بہت لوگ آئے، بہت قصیدے پڑھے گئے جو بہت بڑھیا کاغذ پر چھپے ہوئے ہیں، ساتھ لے آیا ہوں۔ ہمارے سفیر افتخار علی کے علاوہ جو پرانے دوست ہیں، ہندوستان، بنگلہ دیش اور فلسطین کے سفیر بھی آئے، روس کے بڑے Evtushenko اور Vosnozenski جو کہیں اکٹھے نہیں جاتے دونوں آئے اور ہماری نظموں کے روسی ترجمے سنائے۔

Friendship Society کی طرف سے ایک تمغہ بھی ملا، لیکن سب سے زیادہ خوشی یاسر عرفات صاحب کے پیغام سے ہوئی جو ساتھ منسلک ہے۔ کسی عربی دان سے ترجمہ کروالینا، انگلستان میں بہت سی انجمنیں ہیں جن کی آپس میں لڑائی رہتی ہے، سب ۱۳ فروری کے لئے جلسے پر اصرار کر رہے تھے اس لئے ہم نے سب کو منع کر دیا اور چپکے سے برمنگھم چلے گئے جہاں ایک دوست بدر صاحب کے ہاں دوستوں کی محفل ہوئی۔ سلیم شاہد، ضیاء محی الدین اور اس کی بیوی ناہید، ناہید نیازی اور کچھ اور دوست جمع ہوئے۔ بہت سی رسمیں کی گئیں۔ لڑکیوں نے آرتی اتاری۔ گھر والوں نے وزن کر کے گوشت کا صدقہ دیا لیکن افسوس ہے کہ اگلے ہی دن ہمارے پرانے دوست افضل اچانک فوت ہو گئے جس کی وجہ سے اگلے دو تین دن سوگ میں گزرے۔

تمہاری امی ابھی تک سلمٰی کے پاس ہیں اس لئے یہاں تنہائی میں بہت وحشت ہو رہی ہے۔ کل ہمارا بھی وہاں جانے کا ارادہ ہے، اگلے ہفتے ان کے ساتھ لوٹ آئیں گے۔

ڈاکٹر اعجاز کا لندن میں ٹیلیفون آیا تھا لیکن افسوس ہے کہ بات نہ ہو سکی، ہم باہر تھے۔ میری طرف سے میاں بیوی کو پیار پہنچا دینا اور اگر ان کے ابا وہاں ہوں تو انہیں سلام۔

تم نے گھر اور بچوں کے لئے اداسی کا لکھا ہے، وہ تو اپنی جگہ گھر سے باہر ہر کسی کو برداشت کرنی پڑتی ہے۔ لیکن تمہاری جدائی کا زمانہ تو کچھ ایسا لمبا نہیں ہے اور اگر خدا نے چاہا تو ہمارا بھی۔ تم نے ٹکٹ کے پیسوں کے بارے میں پوچھا ہے، اگر تمہاری یونیورسٹی والے مان گئے تو بہت اچھا ہے ورنہ ایک طرف کا ٹکٹ ہمارے ذمے ہے چاہے جتنا بھی ہو، جب وقت آئے تو امی کے بجائے مجھے لکھ دینا۔

بہت سا پیار

ابو

ہم جیتیں گے

حقّا ہم اک دن جیتیں گے
بالآخر اک دن جیتیں گے
کیا خوف ز یلغارِ اعدا
ہے سینہ سپر ہر غازی کا
کیا خوف ز یورش جیش قضا
صف بستہ ہیں ارواح الشہدا
ڈر کاہے کا

ہم جیتیں گے
حقّا ہم اِک دن جیتیں گے
قد جاء الحق وزهق الباطل
فرمودۂ ربِ اکبر
ہے جنت اپنے پاؤں تلے
اور سایۂ رحمت سر پر ہے
پھر کیا ڈر ہے

ہم جیتیں گے
حقّا ہم اک دن جیتیں گے
بالآخر اک دن جیتیں گے

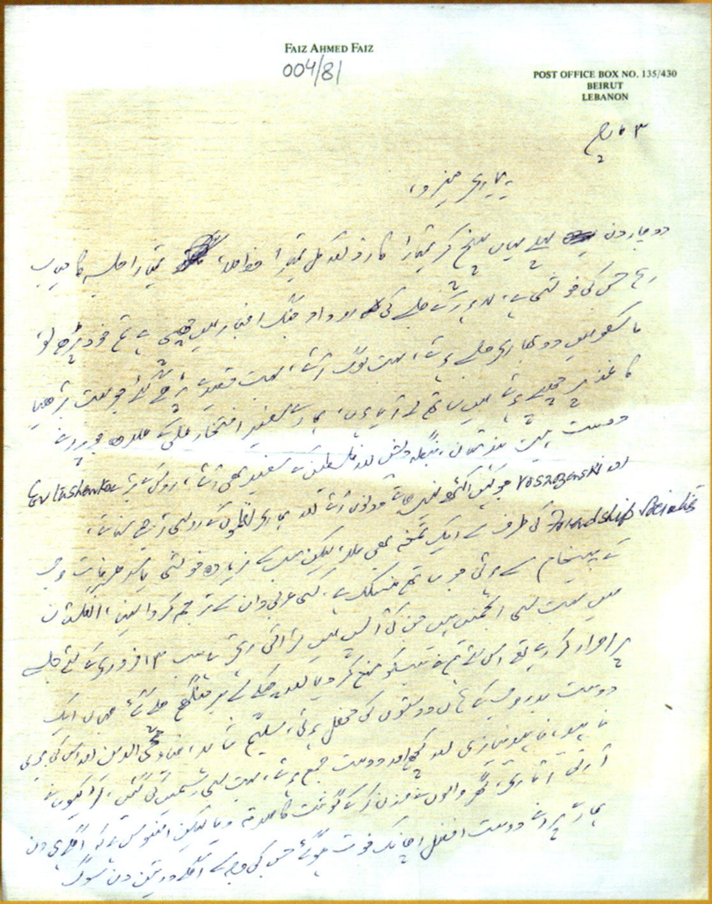
FAIZ AHMED FAIZ

004/81

POST OFFICE BOX NO. 135/430
BEIRUT
LEBANON

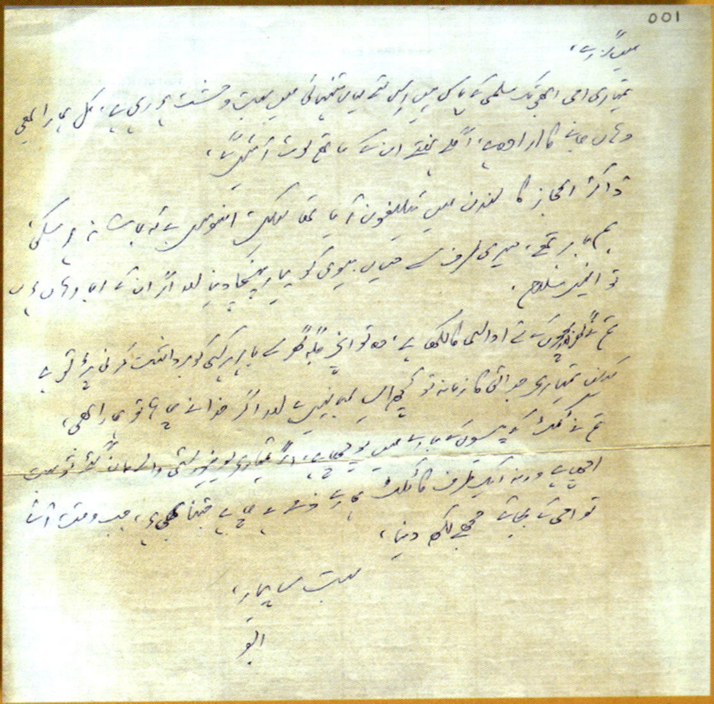
001

اسلام آباد ـــ باكستان منظمة التحرير الفلسطينية

PALESTINE LIBERATION ORGANIZATION ISLAMABAD – PAKISTAN

Date: التاريخ : ـــ

Ref: الرقم : ـــ

Honourable sister,

With a heart filled and with deep sadness, I received the news of the disastrous loss of my brother and friend late Faiz Ahmad Faiz. He was a real Palestinian and International Freedom Fighter. He had a great belief in our people and their just cause and struggle.

It was not enough for him to express his belief in our cause by words but he shared us all our problems by being with us in all the critical times, which faces our revolution and its just cause and during the zionist seige around Beirut he was standing side by side with his brothers, the Palestinians defending the city and the cause and refused to leave us alone facing the zionist aggression.

On my behalf and my brothers in the Executive Committee of the P.L.O., I convey my condolence to your kind and your true beloved two daughters and wish him to lie in peace in the paradise.

YASSIR ARAFAT
Chairman of the Executive Committee of the P.L.O. and the General Leader of the Palestinian Revolution.

Mrs. Allys Faiz Ahmad Faiz.

P.O.BOX No. 1061. Tel: 51389 TELEX No. 5610 P.L.O.PK. ص.ب. ١٠٦١ ـــ هاتف ٥١٣٨٩

I own no property

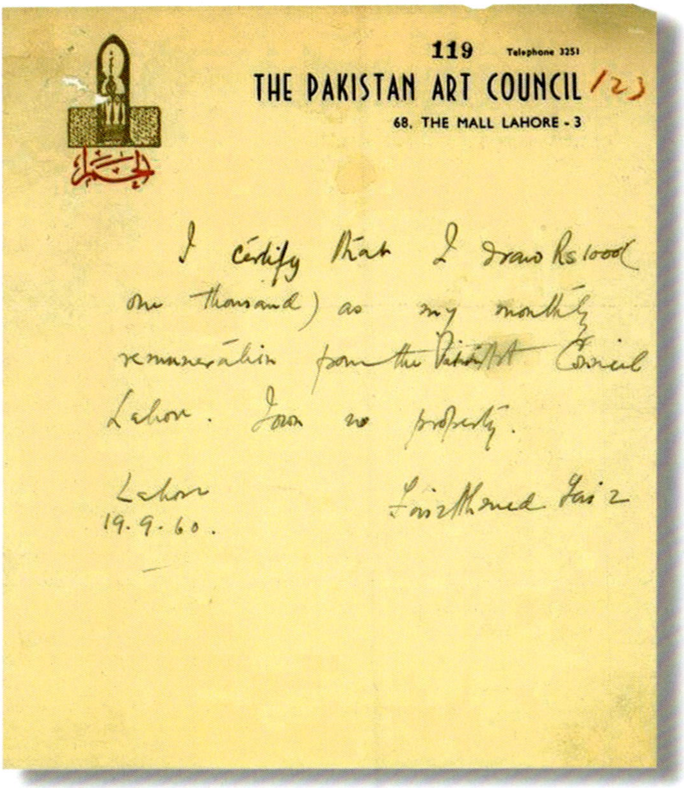

119 Telephone 3251

THE PAKISTAN ART COUNCIL /23

68, THE MALL LAHORE - 3

I certify that I draw Rs 1000 (one thousand) as my monthly remuneration from the Pakistan Art Council Lahore. I own no property.

Lahore
19.9.60.

Faiz Ahmed Faiz

When I read this letter of yours, I was drawn to two statements.
"I draw Rs. 1000/ as my monthly remuneration" and "I own no property".
I kept looking at this letter written sixty years ago, and submitted to The Pakistan Art Council, 68, The Mall Lahore -3, and wondered what prompted you to write it. Was this your tax statement maybe at the time? Rupees one thousand was obviously your monthly salary.

And then the flashbacks started coming.
After finishing my school work I would make my way to the Alhamra in the middle of the afternoon. We lived at 41 Empress Road then. The tall building still stands next to the US Consulate at the end of Empress Road. Ours was the top flat. My walking route took me to the end of the road towards the Governor House, and then along its wall was a katcha nallah (sewage channel). I would meander along carefully until I got to the other end, which brought me out onto Kashmir Road. From there Alhamra was a hop, skip and a jump away, and I would spend my afternoons playing or just messing around. Those were wonderful carefree days.

At that time the building was small and in a crumbling state. The grounds around it were green and huge. Your office, I remember, was at the back of the building, reached by a darkish corridor. The hall, or auditorium at the time, was on the top floor where we also had our music classes. There was a sort of makeshift art studio outside where Aunty Anna Molka and other artists taught painting. In the evening, the place would be abuzz with visitors surrounding the small tea shop type canteen. Artists, actors, dancers and writers would all congregate for gupshup (chitchat) and a smoke. I would just hang around and find someone to talk to until it was close to sun down, and you would send someone to fetch me and we would go home. I remember those days so well. My singing classes with Feroze Nizami and Ameer Haidery gave my lungs and my throat the exercise they needed to belt out the raags (tunes) we were taught. To this day, some notes are still fixed in my memory, although neither the lungs have the capacity nor the throat to recapture them.

When I was offered the post of Chairperson Alhamra in 2019, my first thought was, "What?? But that's where you were". How can I go there with all those memories and your larger than life image still imprinted on my mind.

I must admit I did want to be in the same place as you, not to think for a moment that I could ever even dream of making the difference you did. But the simple thought of following in your footsteps was just so tempting. The thought of having my photograph on the same wall as yours still makes me blink in disbelief. Walking those grounds where your footsteps had trod is another unbelievable experience.
Many people have come to me in these last few months expressing their feelings about the "father-daughter" combo.

Their expectations have been far more than I can ever think of fulfilling. The position of the Chairperson has now changed and is more of a figurehead. It is now the Executive Director, a bureaucrat, who is selected to run the show and has all the financial powers to move things forward.

Infact that in itself is a suitable enough situation for me. Having nothing to do with public money in these times is stressful and also dangerous. There are too many eyes scrutinizing you, too many fingers ready to poke and point, too many nasty and vicious tongues waiting to pounce to discredit you, too many disgruntled persons waiting to air all your dirty linen in public and worst of all, too many negative thoughts within your own conscience to let you move ahead.

Despite all this, I do get that feeling of being a custodian of culture some times. Did you too? But I guess you must have done more about it and actually did, whereas I am trying to walk a difficult narrow path of not compromising on my

One of my most favourite photos

41 Empress Road, Lahore, 2020

commitments and yet not trampling on too many toes at the same time.

Culture today is not how you understood and promoted it. Today it is more of a commercial commodity with hardly any distinction or dignity. The performer is only to be used as and when required. Music is not music as we knew it. It is all about volume and garishness. Melody has vanished.
Theatre is now more about vulgarity and hip shaking. Dance is denied its rightful place. Classical music is hanging on by its finger nails. Instrumentalists are selling motor oil. Their sons are practising rap. Folk artistes are dying out. It is truly a sorry state of affairs.

I took this position only to pay a tribute to your memory and my own desire, nay, read passion, to make a 'difference'. Am I being naïve? Did you take on this job with the same thought, I wonder. Did you not want to make a positive difference, take a step in the right direction, move forward positively and hang the consequences? Were you the risk taker I am?
Sometimes I think you were…

Look at your decision to move to Khadda in Karachi and take over a school and college in an area of druggies, slums and poverty.

To see my photograph next to yours is a culmination of my life's work in promoting culture

It was no small feat setting up the Pakistan National Council of the Arts in rented premises. Today, it is a leading premier institution which is the pride of Pakistan which all international dignitaries visit. Setting up the Classical Cell of music in Radio Pakistan to archive and collect classical music of great masters under one roof. Were these not challenges and risks?

So if I say I want to make a difference where and how I can, I seem to be following your path.

The first Women Festival held on 8th March 2020 at Alhamra was one such example. Hundreds of young women and young men collected to hear sessions on gender-based violence, sports, politics and community development. It was a proud moment for me when the wife of the sitting Governor and the First Lady of Pakistan, Mrs Samina Alvi, agreed to participate at the opening and closing ceremonies.

What is it that I love so much about this place? Is it only my childhood memories that I want to delve back into? Is it the peace and tranquillity I find in my large office, which provides me an opportunity to think, write, create, dream, hide away, relax and be with myself, my most precious companion?

With First Lady of Pakistan Mrs. Samina Alvi
at the First Women Festival, Alhamra 2020

I hear sounds and voices outside which makes me feel that I am in a living space.
When I leave in the evening I see young boys and girls mingling, drinking coffee, playing music sitting on the benches, talking, laughing, just enjoying being alive. They greet me as I leave and I carry their music and laughter with me, throughout my drive home, feeling grateful to have been able to provide them some respite from their otherwise possibly stressful, overworked, and over 'exam-med' lives.
I remember very similar scenes, when I was prancing around as a little girl all those years ago in the same space. Yet the sounds of music, laughter and chattering were very much the same. The groups were smaller in number but the vibes given out were very much the same.

In the conference room, my photograph now hangs on the same wall as yours, though there is a distance between us. You are the first, I am the last so far. Every time I walk by, my heart misses a beat. Do I deserve to be up there with you? Only you can answer that.
And by the way, I don't own any property either!

Discussions we never had, questions I never asked

As I walk along the predetermined path into the twilight of my life, I can afford the luxury of looking back and reconstructing the days gone by. Would I have wanted them any different? Could I have handled the crisis of my life any better? Did I have too many expectations from people and thus felt the betrayals more? Could I have hung on to those moments of happiness for just that bit little longer?

Yes, these would be some of the questions I would have wanted to talk to you about.
You gave so much of your time and energy pursuing causes and ideologies that probably disappointed you in the long run. Did you feel let down or betrayed at the end of a road? Did you ever feel that had you spent this time with your family or friends or living a life of some luxury and ease you might have had less pain and stress? Would your life have been more peaceful and anxiety-free? Would you be watching over your shoulder all those years, or being anxious every time the doorbell rang? Would you have been a happier person if the poverty and injustices of the world around you did not keep you up half the night, trying to frame your emotions into words which expressed that pain, that inner agony, and that clenching of the heart, whilst trying to understand why that was the way it was?

I never asked you why you were in that group, plotting the so-called Rawalpindi Conspiracy which took you away from us for four long years. I never asked you what were you thinking in the cold cell in solitary confinement in the Lahore Fort under death sentence, looking out of a small window. Did you see my face or Cheemie's? Did you think you would never see us again, ever? Did you feel the cold hand of death creeping-up and making you choke? Did you feel anger at the injustice of it all and later the years lost or did you look back and grin about it casually, as was your habit, thinking "water under the bridge"? Time to move on…

As you stood on the dais in Moscow, when they pinned the Lenin Peace Prize on your chest in 1962, did you think, "What did I do to be given this honour? Am I worthy of it? How will I fulfil these expectations in the future?" Your expression in that photograph gives it all away. It is a smile to win all hearts. It is a smile that says it all. Not proud, not "I have arrived", not "Look at me, folks". It is a smile of gentle acceptance and a smile of achievement, and a smile of gratitude. It is a smile that expresses a deep inner strength. This smile became your identity, of your persona that would live on.

Faiz Receiving the Lenin Prize, Moscow 1962

Faiz Receiving the Lenin Prize, Moscow 1962

You met with Yasser Arafat in Beirut many a time, but I never knew about it until I actually saw the photograph where both of you are looking comfortable in each other's company. Your attachment to the Palestinian cause inevitably took me to that troubled part of the world. When I stood at the grave of Yasser Arafat in Ramallah I felt a vibe of camaraderie with this great fighter, a man who took my father to work for a joint cause, a leader who sacrificed his all for his people and their respect for him. I felt a sense of belonging at that moment, not only with the person who lay there, but with the struggle of the entire Palestinian people, a struggle that continues. I wish I could have asked you more about this man, the thoughts he shared with you, and why you followed him to one of the most dangerous places in the world at the time. You faced bomb attacks, violence, killing and then had to escape in the boot of a car to Tunisia. What was it that drew you, or any of us, to follow such ideologies, make our connection with the less fortunate, work for the downtrodden and go on… with "miles to go before I sleep".

Did you, during those days in Beirut, when you had so much time on your hands, reflect and regret taking some of the decisions which were the turning points of your life as you stared at the sea waves beyond your balcony every morning? In those days of longing for home, when you wrote Meray Dil, Meray Musafir (My Heart, My Traveller) which expresses the yearning you felt, did you wish to have lived your life differently, ever?

You met many other intellectuals, celebrities, political leaders, world shapers and so on. What happened during those conversations does not interest me. It's your feelings, your reactions, your responses that I wish I had asked. When you sat across from Gen. Zia ul Haq, the man who caused you the heartache of exile, when you read about the hanging of Bhutto (who at one time was the vision of forward leadership for Pakistan), when you met Pablo Neruda, a poet you admired and respected, when you sat laughing with Ustaad Daman in his Hujra, when you showed Sufi Tabbasum your new poem and waited silently, as he read it and gave his critique as your Ustaad, when you sat in the class of Patras Bokhari as he held you in a trance when he was explaining Keats, when you read about the slaughters across both borders during partition that made you write Yeh dagh dagh Ujala (This tainted dawn) which still resonates today. I remember Mama screaming loudly that fateful morning in Ocober 1958 "Faiz! It's Martial Law!" You came out of your room and your eyes said it all. There was an emptiness in them, a blankness. I was only twelve years old but I knew you were hurting inside and I did not ask you why or how I could help.

Beirut 1979 – Mere Dil, Mere Musafir

Faiz with Pablo Neruda, Sochi 1962

There are photographs of you with the top stars of Bollywood now, sitting at your feet looking longingly at you, with Presidents and Prime Ministers of India holding your hands and hugging you. You are smiling in every one of those, a smile of contentment, is it? Or maybe a thought of bringing peace to both countries, or maybe just a satisfaction that you might have contributed to opening a channel of diplomacy between these two quarrelling neighbours. What you were thinking, I never asked.

The dark days of the long Martial Law of Zia ul Haq took its toll on all of us. You left us for so long, and tried to make a life in London first, then Beirut, only to have to escape in a clandestine manner (since you were a marked man) to Tunisia. I was targeted in my job at PTV constantly: harassed, victimized, chastised publicly for being your daughter. I had so many questions then. Why was this happening to me? Why was my family being driven to despair with transfers of jobs? Why were my boys being treated by their school mates as pariahs because of their grandfather? Where was fairness, transparency and justice? I never got an opportunity to ask those questions either.

On a flight from Lahore to Karachi way back in the 60s, I asked a question which has held me in such good stead through the rest of my life. It was a night coach flight which took more than two hours to reach Karachi. That was the first and last time I ever travelled with you. Perhaps that's why it has stuck in my mind so vividly. I was all of seventeen years or thereabouts. It was a turbulent night. The plane was bucking and jolting. I have been and still am a nervous traveller. I hung onto your arm as if my life depended on it and squeezed it hard to make me feel more secure. You turned to me and said, "Imagine that you are travelling on a rough stony road. The driver has to brake and stop and slow down whenever he sees a stone or boulder on the road. He tries to avoid it as well to make the journey more comfortable for the travellers. This is just a rocky road. The pilot is trying to avoid as many bumps as he can but it will take time before we come to the easier part our journey." I let go of your arm. Suddenly it all made sense. I took a deep breath and put my head on your shoulder as you opened the newspaper. How and when the flight smoothed out I cannot remember. But I know your explanation made it easier for the rest of the journey.

So many people have over the years wanted to know how you wrote, when you wrote, why you wrote, where you wrote, as if I have any of those answers. There are times I see you smoking in the drawing room or in your study, your eyes are not vacant, but focused elsewhere. I know that look well enough not to speak to you. I also sense a restlessness about you. You are not pacing up and down, but there is a general aura around that gives me a feeling that I need to be waiting elsewhere for that time. Now I see your study door has been closed for a while, and know you are in there but want to be alone with your thoughts and the words that are flowing from your pen. I was never the one who saw the first draft of the creation, but I remember how proudly you brought the first edition of your Kuliyaaat and gave me and Humair a copy just before you departed for your final abode in November 1984. Your smile said it all.

Now that your poems are recited all over the world, creating bonding between people and groups who strongly identify, not only with the words, but with the poet and his vision, did you know this would happen as you were writing them? Did you feel the words would resonate for decades after you had left? Did you realize that your words would give courage to so many incarcerated in their cold cells waiting for any glimmer of hope? Did you imagine freedom marches across continents holding up banners which had your verses? Did you ever think your words would be quoted by those very people who denied your freedom of thought and speech and pushed you into self-exile? Again more questions I never asked...

And then the happy moments when we were together, as a family, the sheer joy on your face, surrounded by your grandchildren, is what makes it all worth the agony of separation which I had to endure growing up, during your exile, and your many, many travels which took you away from me...
I missed you then...
I miss you now...
I will miss you until my last breath...

But be prepared I will ask my questions when we meet again, and there will be all the time in the world and I will seek all the answers.
Until then, rest in peace Abbu...

Letter

003 / 81
Beirut, Lebanon

Dear Mizu,

Your letter after many days. You may not be able to do anything about the other matters but it is important to take care of your health. If the doctors say so then take a few days off to rest, although that too is not an easy thing to do in your 'zoo'. If you are so fed up of your work, then let that go also. Now you have a degree. Teaching will bring in less money but that also means less work. If you won't be eating meat, then let it be lentils. Peace of mind is better than money. But if you can be patient, that would be the best. If circumstances can turn bad they can also improve at some stage.... 'in vicissitudes of fortune are the seven skies, ever'. April is here and if the Americans behave properly it would be good.

We are both comfortable but want to see you all dearly. I hope there will be some way we can meet this year. I am sending the things your friends asked for.

Lots of love,
Abbu

Letter

005 /80
Beirut, Lebanon
11 April

Dear Mizu,

I had just written to you when I received your second letter. Made me very happy.
As I had written, there can be no solution to office problems so, as far as possible apply my 'switch off' prescription. A better prescription is that given by Malik Feroze Khan Noon but then perhaps that can only be applied by very senior officials. When I was in Delhi, Malik Saheb was the Member Defence of the Viceroy's Council. One day I and Bokhari senior went to see him in his office. What do we see? That there is not a single piece of paper on Malik Saheb's table and he is smoking a cigar with not a care in the world! Bokhari Saheb said, "Malik Saheb there is a war going on, you are the Member Defence and here you are doing no work." Malik Saheb replied, "Shah Jee, don't talk about work. The more you do it the more it expands. So I just don't work."
It made me happy to learn about the children's exams and the spring in the garden at home, though the very thought saddens my heart. The consolation is that one day I shall come and see it for myself.

And what is this rubbish about paying back? You and I are not strangers. The only relationship to pay back is of love. That we continue to love each other. I might need your help if I have to live another ten, twenty years and if I become handicapped. In that case I shall go back to the village where the 'Mirasi' will keep refilling my pipe and his wife the 'Mirasan' will press my feet.

Lots of love to everybody,
Abbu

خط

003 / 81
Beirut, Lebanon

پیاری میزو،

بہت دنوں کے بعد تمہارا لمباخط ملا۔ دوسرے حالات پر تو اپنا اختیار نہیں البتہ اپنی صحت کے بارے میں احتیاط ضروری ہے۔ اگر ڈاکٹر کہتے ہیں تو بہتر یہی ہے کہ کچھ دن چھٹی لے کر آرام کرو اگر چہ تمہارے چڑیا گھر میں یہ بھی کچھ آسان بات نہیں۔ اگر اپنے کام سے دل بہت تنگ آ گیا ہے تو اس سے بھی چھٹی کرو۔ اب تمہارے پاس ڈگری تو موجود ہے، پڑھانے کے کاروبار میں پیسے کم ملیں گے لیکن کام بھی تو کم ہوگا۔ گوشت نہ سہی دال روٹی سہی۔ پیسے سے سکون بہتر ہے۔ اگر صبر ہو سکے تو وہ بھی ٹھیک ہے۔ حالات اگر بدتر ہو سکتے ہیں تو کبھی نہ کبھی بہتر بھی ہو سکتے ہیں، 'رات دن گردش میں ہیں سات آسماں'۔ اپریل کا مہینہ شروع ہو چکا ہے۔ اگر امریکہ والے کچھ شرافت کریں تو سب سے اچھا ہے۔

ہم دونوں آرام سے ہیں البتہ تم سب کو دیکھنے کے لئے دل بے قرار رہتا ہے۔ امید ہے اس سال کسی نہ کسی صورت ملنا ہو ہی جائے گا۔ تمہارے دوستوں کے لئے ان کی فرمائش بھیج رہا ہوں۔

بہت سا پیار

ابو

خط

005 /80
Beirut, Lebanon
11 April

پیاری میزو

تمہیں ایک خط لکھا ہی تھا کہ تمہارا دوسرا خط آ گیا۔ بہت خوشی ہوئی۔

دفتری دردِ سر کا تو جیسے میں نے لکھا تھا کوئی علاج نہیں۔ جہاں تک ہو سکے ہمارا switch off والا نسخہ استعمال کرنا چاہیئے۔ اس سے بھی اچھا نسخہ مرحوم ملک فیروز خان نون کا ہے، لیکن وہ شاید صرف بڑے افسر استعمال کر سکتے ہیں۔ وہ نسخہ یہ ہے کہ جب ہم دہلی میں تھے تو ملک صاحب وائسرائے کی کونسل کے ڈیفنس ممبر تھے۔ ایک دن میں اور بڑے بخاری دفتر مین ان سے ملنے گئے۔ دیکھا کہ ملک صاحب کی میز پر ایک بھی کاغذ نہیں اور وہ ہاتھ پر ہاتھ دھرے چرٹ پی رہے ہیں۔ بخاری صاحب نے کہا، ملک صاحب لڑائی ہو رہی ہے اور آپ ڈیفنس ممبر ہیں آپ کو کوئی کام نہیں ہے۔ ملک صاحب بولے، (شاہ جی، کم دا نہ پچھو، جتنا کرو انہا ای ودھدا اے، ایس لئی کری دا ای نئیں)۔

بچوں کے امتحانات سے خوشی ہوئی اور تمہارے اور اپنے گھر کے باغوں پر بہار آنے سے بھی۔ اگر چہ اس کے تصور سے دل اداس بھی ہوتا ہے۔ لیکن اتنی تسکین کہ کبھی آ کر دیکھ بھی لیں گے۔

اور یہ احسان چکانے کی کیا بکواس ہے جیسے ہم تم کوئی الگ الگ چیز ہیں، ہمارا تمہارا احسان یہی ہے کہ پیار کرتے رہیں، اور خدمت کرنے کی ضرورت تو شاید جب پڑے گی اگر اور دس بیس برس جینا پڑا اور ہاتھ پاؤں جواب دے گئے، پھر تو ہم گاؤں چلے جائیں گے، جہاں میراثی حقہ بھرا کرے گا اور میراثن پاؤں دبایا کرے گی۔

سب کو بہت سا پیار

ابو

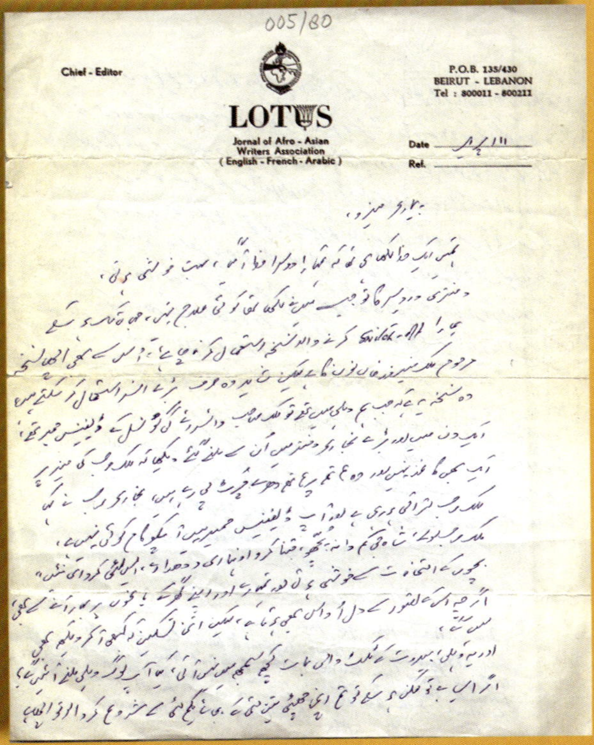

005/80

Chief - Editor

LOTUS

Jornal of Afro - Asian Writers Association (English - French - Arabic)

P.O.B. 135/430
BEIRUT - LEBANON
Tel : 800011 - 800211

Date ۱۱/ ۱۱

Ref.

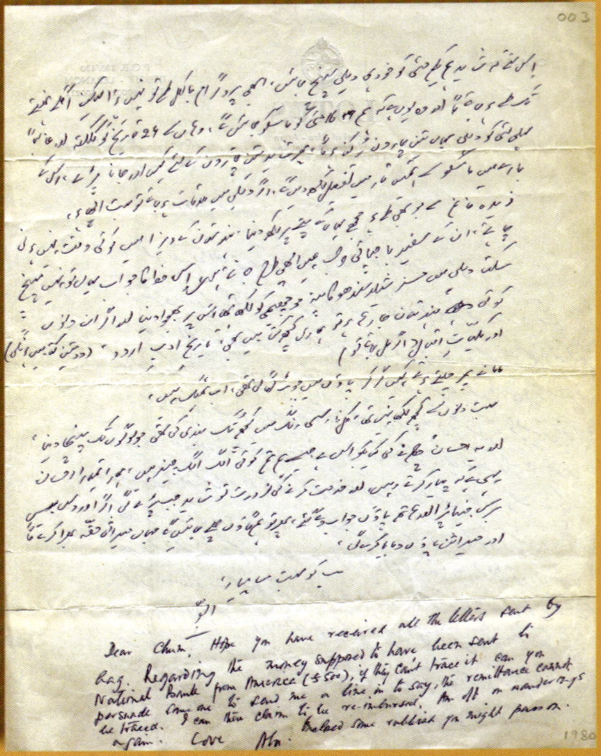

003

Dear Chum. Hope you have received all the letters sent by Rag. Regarding the money supposed to have been sent to National Bank from America ($500), if they can't trace it can you persuade someone to send me a line in to say, the remittance cannot be traced. I can then claim to be re-imbursed. Am off in a few days again. Love Abu. Enclosed some rubbish you might process.

1980

Actual Letters

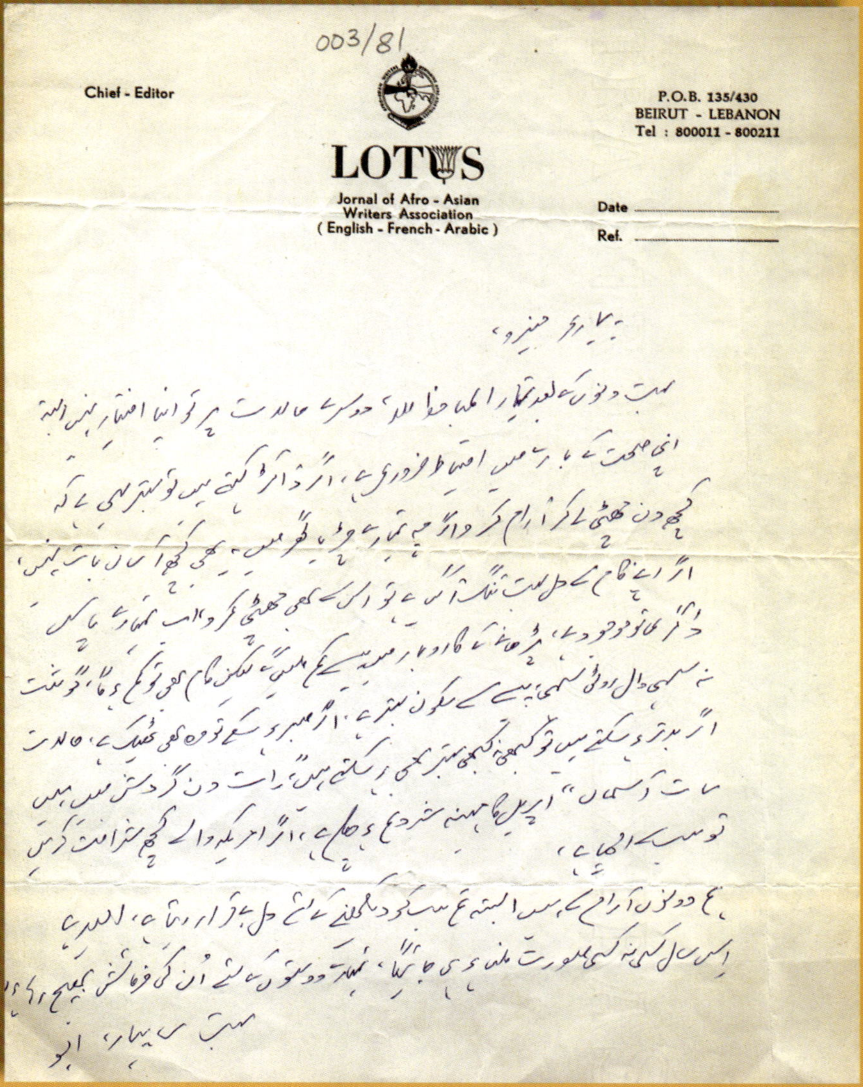

003/81

Chief - Editor

LOTUS

Jornal of Afro - Asian
Writers Association
(English - French - Arabic)

P.O.B. 135/430
BEIRUT - LEBANON
Tel : 800011 - 800211

Date ______________

Ref. ______________

پیاری میزو،

بہت دنوں کے بعد تمہارا خط ملا۔ دوسرے معاملات پر تو اپنا اختیار نہیں البتہ
اپنی صحت کے بارے میں احتیاط ضروری ہے۔ اگر ڈاکٹر کہتے ہیں تو بہتر یہی ہے کہ
کچھ دن چھٹی لے کر آرام کرو اگرچہ تمہارے ہاں گھر میں یہ بھی کچھ آسان بات نہیں،
اگر اس کام سے دل بہت تنگ آ گیا ہے تو اس سے بھی چھٹی کرو۔ اب تمہارے پاس
[illegible]
[illegible]
[illegible]
[illegible]
[illegible]
[illegible]

یہ دونوں آرام سے ہیں البتہ تم سب کو دیکھنے کے لئے دل بے قرار رہتا ہے۔ اللہ نے
اس سال کسی نہ کسی صورت ملنا ہو ہی جائے گا۔ [illegible]

بہت سے پیار، ابو

People say I look and smile like you